IN SEARCH OF CALM

Renewal for a Mother's Heart

By Elisabeth K. Corcoran

© 2005

Elisabeth K. Corcoran

Contents

Acknowledgements

This book has come out of a different stretch of life for me than my first one. My kids are older...my marriage is older...my friendships are older...my faith is older... which I guess means, *I'm* older. I'm hoping I'm at least a bit wiser too. These things could only get older with the passing of time...and these things could only get stronger with the mysterious combination of effort on my part and grace on God's part...a lot of grace.

So thank you, Sara and Jack, for allowing me to write about you – though I don't think you actually know that I do that for a living yet. And thank you for giving me such great material, also unbeknownst to you. I thank God that He changed my heart all those years ago and gave me a desire to have you two.

Thank you, Kevin, for healing with me and for working hard to get us to a place that is safe and just plain good for both of us. I am so grateful for your willingness to let me do so many things that I love to do. But I am even more grateful that at the end of the day, we come home to each other.

Thank you to each of my friends...'the girls' who I promised I would list if you promised to pray for this book!

— Deb Hardison, Keely Robertson, Erika Solgos, Parker Vander Ploeg and Michelle Venhuizen...you fill my soul...you take care of me and you let me take care of you...and I love you all more than I will ever be able to say this side of heaven...what would I do without you?!

Thank you to my second family and probably my favorite place on earth (next to my home) — Blackberry Creek Community Church. Over eleven years later, I love you all more and more every day. And thanks to Eric Vander Ploeg, my pastor, boss and friend, who always pushes me to be better than what I think I can be.

Thank you, Gramma & Grampa Klein, for providing the means and the encouragement all those years ago to fulfill this dream of mine. I miss you, but I know you are enjoying each other and Jesus together.

And thank You, my Heavenly Father, who has stayed close even when I wandered, and who has been and will always be my closest Friend. I love You more now than the first night I met You...and I trust You more now than ever before.

This book is dedicated to my Mom...who I am ecstatic to say now 'gets it'. I love you.

Introduction

Life is funny. Just when you think you've got it all figured out, something surprising comes along. Like kids, for instance. You think you can prepare. You buy yourself different clothes for that short season when your body is overtaken by something otherworldly. You register for things you think you'll need. You hear horror stories about other women's birth experiences (what is that, by the way? why do we women feel compelled to scare first-time pregnant women half to death with details no one really wants to know?). You read books. You take classes. You learn the right way to breathe, sit, eat and sleep. You prepare the nursery. You count your protein grams and drink water like it's going out of style. You see the doctor more than the rest of your life combined. You use the bathroom more often than you can keep track. You crave foods that you've never eaten before. You get weighed more than any woman should ever have to be weighed. You endure an endless string of unsolicited sound bytes of advice, from complete strangers I might add. You even give stuff up that formerly you couldn't imagine your life without (like caffeine, candy, laying around doing nothing for long periods of time). Not to mention the ever present hand just waiting to rub your belly like it's a little Buddha statue and you're in the good luck dispensing business.

But then they come. First of all – the way they arrive into our lives should be an indication of what to expect from them. It all starts with the strangest, rawest, and let's be honest, most painful physical experience of our lives. But then they are put into our arms. Looking back, both of my children's personalities were already formed by those first few moments together. My daughter, Sara – my anal retentive, high maintenance, firstborn girly girl through and through – began by simply screaming for what seemed like an eternity. Yep, that's about right. And my son, Jack – well, I have this picture of us just seconds after he was born, looking up right into my eyes, Mr. Laid Back, as if to say, 'hey Mom, what's up?' They come out of our body, or somebody else's on our behalf, and then they weasel their way right into our hearts. *How do they do that?* And we find that we're never the same again.

My daughter, now 8, just asked me the other day, 'Were you lonely before Jack and I came along?' How do I answer that? Do I tell her that there was a time when I didn't even want children? Do I tell her how I used to be able to do so much more of what I wanted to do before they came along? Do I tell her how my life is not the same anymore and I barely even remember what life was like before them? No...I tell her the day she came into my life, something in my heart said 'yes'...like I had been waiting for something that I didn't even know had been missing up til then. Because though being a mom is hard and time-consuming and not always the most fun thing in the world...my heart is different now. I am different now. And I like the me that God has created me to be through my kids way more than the old me.

But yet...I am still on that search for Calm. At times I think it is just about the most illusive thing out there. And other times, when I find myself sitting quietly on the couch with a cup of hot chocolate and a magazine, I think I've figured it out. But that's just it. I'm not looking for the Calm then. I mean, those moments are wonderful and sweet, don't get me wrong. But the Calm I am looking for is the kind that I can grab hold of when the bell's going to ring in 5 minutes and I just realized the kids didn't brush their teeth yet and I forgot to sign that permission slip. I need Calm then. Or when one of my kids digs in their heels and won't budge on something that I think is desperately important for them to obey me on. I need Calm then. Or when my world comes crashing down around me, either through a relational wrong or a circumstantial tragedy, and I don't know how to take the next breath – *I need Calm then.*

What I hope to encourage you with is this...though an hour of solitude is a wonderful thing (and you really should try it!)...you can find God in the everyday. He is already there, in fact. So what we need are spiritual eyes to see what He is already doing and already saying.

And I am amazed at how God, my Calm, keeps showing up and teaching me things and reminding me that He is with me and that I am His and that I am loved more than I'll ever understand. And if you stop reading right here, you've gotten my whole point.

1

Grace in the Most Unlikely Places

*If we confess our sins, He is faithful and just
And will forgive us ours sins and purify us from all
unrighteousness.*
I John 1:9

I did it again! I swear, I just can't seem to get this mothering thing down sometimes. Sara was simply in my way as I was trying to walk across the kitchen...this wasn't deliberate disobedience on her part, by any means. And I yelled at her. The feeling in the pit of my stomach when I do that – it just makes me sick.

Okay, so I had a few options right at that moment. Pretend I didn't just snap at her for no reason and move on with life.

Start beating myself up for being a lousy mother.

Or fix it.

Well, if I did the pretending game, then I would have taught my daughter a couple things. One, you can be mean to someone and not have to apologize for it. And I would have been basically saying to her that she wasn't a very important person. Neither of those lessons were ones I wanted to pass on.

I could have gone the guilt route. Heaping a weight on my shoulders that left me feeling unfit to mother Sara. Carrying around blame much longer than necessary and therefore turning my day into a waste of time.

Or I could have taken care of the situation. And, thankfully, at that moment, I chose this high road. (Unfortunately, I don't always…) I went to Sara, knelt down, looked her in the eyes, and said, "I am sorry for yelling at you and hurting your feelings. Mommy was wrong." She said, "I forgive you, Mommy. I was frustrated with you, too." (Ahh, the honesty of a child…) Then I took it a step farther. I then asked God for His forgiveness and asked Him for patience and help the next time I was about to lose it.

I felt better almost instantly after taking care of it that way. Confess, repent, move on. The lesson I taught my daughter in that moment was that yes, mommy is human and will mess up a lot; however, it can be made right when you choose to, and you can be granted forgiveness and a clean slate.

And I was reminded yet again that my daughter and my God are very forgiving.

Personal Touch

Commit right now – that the next time you lose it with one of your children (and there *will* be a next time – we're only human!) – that you will put into practice the high road steps I've suggested – confess to God and to your child, repent (prayerfully promise to work at it not happening again – or so soon – or to that same degree – or over something that little, etc.), then move on. You'll be pleased at your efforts to show a desire to grow in your mothering and in your holiness…and so will God.

Prayer

Dear God, Thank You for Your promise to wash us clean if only we come to You and acknowledge our wrongs. You are so full of grace! Amen.

2

Let the Little Ones Go to Him

"Therefore, whoever humbles {herself} like a child is the greatest in the kingdom of heaven."
Matthew 18:4

Sara had asked to pray before breakfast this morning. That is quite typical of her. I think it's more her penchant to take charge than her avid spiritual growth as of yet. But I happily obliged as it still does something to my heart to hear that little girl of mine talk to our Heavenly Father.

She started off per usual. *Thank You for mommy, thank You for daddy, thank You for Jack.* Then she added, *And thank You for me.* She has yet to come across that place in life where you feel silly or full of yourself in bringing any sort of attention to who you are as a person. As adults, we'd probably be a bit taken aback to hear a fellow pray-er at our Bible study thank God for herself. But if you think about it...I think the situation is less that she hasn't quite learned prayer etiquette, and more that she may know more than we as grown-ups do. Why *not* thank God for ourselves? He made us as much as He made the other people we thank Him for. We have as much value as those other people do. And I bet, if we began to sprinkle our prayers every now and then with a small 'thank you for me', I just bet we'd start to see our value though His eyes. And that wouldn't be such a bad thing.

She then moved on to the rest of her list of thanks. Sara has not yet progressed much past the thanksgiving kind of prayers. She doesn't ask God for anything. She doesn't confess much either. (That will need to come...) She just thanks Him. And today, I noticed exactly what she was thanking Him for. She went through her routine of thanking Him for breakfast, and her pretty clothes, and *thank You that I'm beautiful again today* (no self-esteem issues with this little girl). But then I heard her saying, *And thank You for dolly needing to be fixed and...* Did you catch that? Because I almost didn't. She didn't *ask* God to fix her dolly. She simply thanked Him for her dolly dilemma. Now, I'm sure she wasn't hoping to teach me some huge theological lesson in that moment...but wow, did she ever. What if I stopped, just for a day even, asking God for stuff? Asking Him to fix things in my life? Asking Him to change this or that circumstance? What if – what if I just thanked Him for all of my situations as is? How might my life be different? How might I see God and my current status differently...if instead of complaining to Him or asking Him for a quick-fix, I just rested where I was at that moment...searching for His hand and for any lesson I could glean...and thanked Him for it?

Maybe I'll just have to find out.

Personal Touch

Find out today. Right this minute. Put the book down and quiet your heart. I want you to spend time in prayer – but not just any kind of prayer. Pure thanksgiving. Ask God to open your eyes and heart to answered prayer around you – now begin to thank Him for every blessing you have been given…and every circumstance you wish you could wriggle yourself out of. You have no idea how an attitude of thanks will change your perspective on your situation.

Prayer

Dear God, I thank You for being holy and merciful and loving. I thank You for thinking me up and creating me. I thank You for loving me so completely. I thank You for the gift of life. I thank You for my husband. I thank You for my children. I thank You for the place I call home. I thank You for all the good things in my life. And I thank You for all the circumstances that You are allowing so that I might find growth. Amen.

3

I'm the One in the Middle

We are hard-pressed on every side, but not crushed;
perplexed, but not in despair;
persecuted, but not abandoned; struck down,
but not destroyed.
II Corinthians 4:8-9

I didn't like being a mother today. And I'm not talking about simply being frustrated. It was one thing after another with both of my kids. And I believe I outright said at one point (under my breath) – "I want to give up mothering permanently."

Could this be PMS? *Possibly.* Could it have been circumstantial? *Maybe.* Could I have been tired? *Perhaps.* Have I neglected spending time with God lately? *Conceivably.* Are any of these excuses my point? *Nope.*

I have this feeling more times than I want to admit –

mothering does not always come naturally to me. I almost feel as if I should confess this to God and ask for forgiveness. And sometimes I do. Because I feel guilty. It doesn't feel right. It doesn't feel like something I should be feeling (especially as an author of a book on encouraging weary mothers!). But I *do* feel this way. This ache. This 'I-have-so-many-things-I-want-to-do-with-my-life (-but-I-can't-quite-yet-because-I'm-a-mother)' feeling that haunts me at times.

And I felt for so long that I couldn't even utter these words out loud. What kind of woman and mother would I be if I didn't always particularly even *like* being a mother? Well, I figured – since there's nothing new under the sun, that also goes for my feelings. Chances are I am not the first woman in the world to feel this way – to feel this at-times detachment, this intangible longing, this indescribable discontentment. At least, I hope I'm not.

I have this theory that there are three kinds of women. There's the woman who has always known (like, from birth) that she has wanted to be a mother – and she is fantastic at it, thriving in this role. (In fact, for her, it's not a role – it is who she is to the core.) On the other end of the spectrum is the woman (also, almost from birth) who has always known that she did *not* want to be a mother – and she finds her womanly fulfillment in a myriad of other ways throughout her life. Then there's the other one in the middle somewhere – the one who wants to be a mom, but is the kind that does not automatically love all children (she loves hers completely and cares infinitely for the children of her friends and extended family, but that's about the extent of it). For her, mothering is amazing, but not necessarily the defining factor in her life.

I have always candidly believed I have fallen into the middle category. I love my kids – but this mothering thing can sort of rub me the wrong way sometimes. Requiring much more selflessness than I ever would have guessed and much more than I seem to have at my disposal to dole out. I have these longings – to do so much more, to be so much more...a longing to still be the one being taken care of, instead of the consummate caregiver...

Yes, I have dreams. Some will wait for me and my season of life to change. And some will not. Yes, I have yearnings and discontentments that drive me to question my commitment to my children. But something I know for sure – I have been handed two children. God could have chosen a childless life for me. But, for whatever reason, He didn't. He, the Creator and Guide of my life, knew the best goals for my life and the best ways to get me there. And He knows my struggles – inside and out – and He is just waiting for me to hand them back over to Him.

And so that is what I must do. Do the next thing – take the next step – wake up the next day and meet my children's needs. All the while – allowing God to walk with me and bring me closer to what He wants me to be, which technically should be my ultimate goal and dream anyway. So I'll chase after that dream – the one that can be attained no matter the season of life...

Personal Touch

So, which person are you? Are you in love with being a mother? That is fantastic! Thank God for it! Were you one of those who vowed they'd never have babies, and now you find yourself with one on each hip? God can get you through this – and I bet He has grown your heart into complete love for the children He's given you. Or are you like me – in the middle? God made you that way – don't begrudge it. Accept it and move on. You are a mom now and He can create in you a heart that nurtures your kids, while giving you a glimpse of a hope and a future that will allow you to fulfill some of those other dreams swirling in the back of your head.

Prayer

Dear God, Wow – I am a mom! How did that happen? Why did You choose me to do this? Well, You are all-knowing, so I need to simply trust that I have been given these children for a reason...because You know, that with Your strength, I can do this well. Amen.

4

Outwitted Again?!

If any of you lacks wisdom,
{she} should ask God, who gives generously
to all without finding fault,
And it will be given to {her}.
James 1:5

I just did one of the stupidest things ever. As if someone else, I watched myself angrily put black suede sparkled boots on my daughter's feet because she actually refused to brush her teeth without donning some type of footwear. We were in the midst of a battle – I could think of no proper choices to give her – I couldn't seem to stay the one in control – and she won. She won this dispute. I walked out of the room after watching her happily brush her teeth, boot-clad, just shaking my head, wondering where she got this will of iron.

Funny, my husband would insist she got it from me. He says it with a smile and a twinkle in his eye, but I swear that he almost believes that one day I took Sara aside, sat her down and said, 'this is how you can get your way for the rest of your life', and proceeded to give her my tricks of the trade. But as far as I can recall, that never actually happened.

So was it osmosis? She sees me walk around on a daily basis wielding my power as woman-hear-me-roar, and decided that she wanted the same kind of clout herself? Let's think this through just a bit – if that were truly the case, wouldn't I probably have my hands full just abit more with my gentle-spirited son as well? But I don't. It's just with Sara.

So is it a mother-daughter thing that started at 10 months? Do I have a lifetime of battle-choosing and battle-losing ahead of me? Do I have to lay down my mothering muscle at the foot of my daughter because somehow she is able to outsmart me a good portion of the time?

You'd think I was gearing up to answer myself here – but I'm not. I am clueless.

You know, the other day, I reminded Sara to make her bed before coming downstairs (an act that she normally must do because it drives her nuts to have her room undone in any fashion). But this particular day, she said, 'I don't want to make my bed today.' Taken aback, I said, 'Sara, you have two choices…you can either make your bed now or…' And I was stumped. My mind could not come up with an alternative…I wasn't going to make her stay home from church that day, nor was I going to withhold breakfast if she didn't comply. So I took a deep breath, stalling, and repeated, 'Sara, your choices are that you can either make your bed or…ummm…you can make your bed or…' And she looked at me, sighed, and said, 'Mommy, why don't I just make my bed?' My lack of quick thinking had apparently bored my daughter into obedience. Sadly, it wasn't so much that she desired to please me – she was simply uninterested in watching me deliberate so long. I may have won the battle that time, but I'm not so sure if by default really counts.

Outwitted again…ahhh, but it mustn't be like this for the long haul. Yes, she may prevail in a clash here and there – but our God has given me authority as her parent…and occasionally, when I actually think to ask for it, He gives me creativity and wisdom. She may win in the moment from time to time – but she doesn't see what I see – that I am attempting to train her for a life that is built on something much bigger than getting her own way. And for that, God is on my side.

Personal Touch

Next time you're in the heat of a battle with one of your kids (you know, like over the important, life and death stuff, like whether or not they'll wear their raincoat to school or eat all their green beans!), take a huge, deep breath and ask yourself – is this a fight I really want and need to pursue?

Prayer

Dear God, I need Your wisdom! This is so much harder than I ever thought it would be. Please teach me how to be a mother! Amen.

5

I'm Settling In

There is a time...
to embrace and a time to refrain.
Ecclesiastes 3:1b&5b

My Sara just asked me the other day if I would give her money for college. I asked her to clarify if she meant spending money or if she wanted to know if Daddy & I were putting money away for her education. She said she was interested in the latter. I assured her that we were, and that seemed to satisfy her curiosity. But now my curiosity was piqued. Where does my daughter come up with this stuff? She's not even in preschool yet and she wants to talk college.

I must admit that this tiny little question made my mind wander down the road about 14 or so years to the time when she's actually heading off. On this end, it seems like ages away. But I've been told a number of times, just recently in fact, that it goes *so fast*...to truly remember how much my kids love me right now, because they won't always act like they love me later. I do know that time goes fast – I cannot believe that it's been over 5 years since finding out that I was pregnant with Sara...and now look, she's getting ready for preschool, gets dressed by herself, needs little help in hopping up into her booster carseat and buckling herself in, and is even pondering her higher education plans.

But I've been reminded (and warned) that this is just the beginning...first days of school, bullies, dance lessons, questions that will knock me off my feet, waiting up into the night for her to come home, driving, dating, broken hearts...basically letting go a little more each day until one day when she really does jump into her own car that she will have purchased after getting her own after school job (and a little help from mom and dad because of all those straight A's!) into the sunset towards college and a future that does not hold a daily dose of her mommy and daddy anymore.

So, I think I'll settle in for the right now...the time that I so desperately want to rush through because it can be so tiring and frustrating sometimes...I want to just remember these precious moments. It won't be long before both Sara and Jack stop jumping into my lap, stop running to kiss and hug me each morning, stop holding my hand on purpose and without embarrassment, stop telling me ten times a day that they love me...but for now they still do...and I want to remember.

Personal Touch

Grab your calendar and promise me this – mark off one weekday each week this month that you will stay home all day long. Then once you have those four days in place for this coming month: on one day, mark that you'll turn off the phone; one day, turn off the television; one day, turn off the radio; and on one day, try turning all of them off! Now before those days hit you (and a fear being bored out of your mind overwhelms you!), pray and plan. Pray for creativity and plan activities for just you and your kids. These years go fast – but you can capture them and help to make the time linger a bit.

Prayer

Dear God, I want to love just being a mom for now. Please grow that desire in me to follow the calling You've laid out for my life at this special and precious season. Amen.

6

Even When I Don't Remember

God is our refuge and strength,
An ever-present help in trouble.
Psalm 46:1

Sara and I have just returned home from her annual physical…shots and all…in preparation for her starting school. And I cannot believe that my baby is starting school this year. I love this time of year – not really the temperature changes necessarily – but there is just something about preparing for the school year and the ministry year that gets me excited.

My husband is a 6th grade teacher, so we have lived on the school calendar year long before our kids came along. My life kicks into a different sort of gear when he heads back to work and I'm up against the ominous task of stay at home parenting on my own again. Every year I know I am ready for my husband to go back to work (3 months can be a lot of one-on-one time in our marriage!), but every year I sort of step back, eye my children, and wonder – will I really be able to pull this off for another 9 months? Do I have what it takes to let the change of seasons take me farther down the road of life? Can I juggle full-time stay-at-home wifery/mothering/homemaking with ministry and writing (and keep my sanity?)?

And my answer, my friends, is an unequivocal no. I cannot juggle all of that and remain mentally healthy. And I do not have within me what it takes to go with the flow of life on my own. Nope, uh-uh, not me. But I do know someone who can juggle for me, and who does have what it takes within Him. God.

When I was asked to do my first speaking engagement a while back, I remembered the story of Moses being asked by God to help free His people. (Not really a close comparison of tasks, but...) Moses replied, *Who am I? God, I am not a great man.* Basically, why me? Sounds familiar...I think things like that all the time. *Who am I to speak in public and try to encourage women when my own life can be such a mess sometimes? What were you thinking, God, to put me in charge of the care of these two little kids? I nowhere near have my act all together.* And I was so struck by God's response. He didn't give Moses a peptalk, He didn't cheerlead him into the task, and He didn't point out all the wonderful things about him, all the reasons he could handle this task. His answer was simply this, I'll tell you why you can do this...because I will be with you.

And He says that to you and me today as we doubt our abilities to be a good wife and a good mother and a good friend and a good daughter and...you get my point...when we wonder how in the world we will get through the next day, let alone do it with some mastery...God says – I'll tell you why and how you can do all of these things...because I will be with you. If you just ask.

There are days that I forget that truth completely. I forget that God is with me. I forget that He is not just with me when I remember that He is, but all the time. I forget that I have His strength not just to lean on – but that His strength will be the strength that gets me through each day.

But there are days that I remember His presence. And I can feel my shoulders untense, and my forehead unfurrow, and my soul let out a sigh of relief. My prayer is that I have more of those days – when I remember that I am not in this all alone...that I have a fully competent Helper by my side at all times.

He is with me right now as I write this. And He is with you, if you have entered into a relationship with His Son, right now as you read this. So, rest assured – you do not have to juggle. You do not have to do it all in your own strength. If you so desire and if you so ask, God can and will be the Strength that will get you through the ebb and flow of this ever-changing life.

Personal Touch

Let's practice His presence today. More than likely, you'll need to plan ahead. Take a look at your week, and pencil in (no, make that *pen* in) one hour when you can be completely alone with God. Bring your Bible and a notebook along. Ask God to reveal Himself to you. Then wait in passionate expectation for Him to show up.

Prayer

Dear God, This time is just for You and me. Please help me to feel You and hear You now. Please ease my soul. And please make me much more aware of Your Presence in the day to day. Amen.

7

God's Way or Your Way?

*Come near to God
And He will come near to you.*
James 4:8

Jack and Sara were playing in our backyard on the swingset. My husband had installed a new swing (think Tim-the-Toolman-Taylor and his quest for everything to have more power). Now, of course, both kids want to swing in the new swing each time. (We were better off without that 'improvement'!)

And I heard the beginnings of what was about to be a very interesting conversation. Sara began to lecture Jack, as Jack had beaten her to the swing. 'You know, Jack,' she said, hands on her hips, 'you could do this *God's* way or *your* way. God's way is sharing. Don't you want to do it God's way, Jack?'

Funny how it never even crossed her mind that God's way probably more so translated to her waiting her turn patiently. But what do you expect from a little kid who wants her swing? Jack's answer, of course, a simple, right-to-the-point, 'My way,' and he kept on swinging.

I had to intervene before God's way turned into something reminiscent of an Old Testament battle. So I made the above suggestion to Sara, which she quickly discounted as viable, and after realizing whining was not getting her anywhere, promptly went on to stealing Jack's bike in the hopes of getting him off the swing. It worked. Sara's version of God's way prevailed.

But that got me thinking (as most of what Sara and Jack say tends to). Two thoughts came to mind: How often do I choose, either out of blatant selfishness or outright lack of truth, my way over God's way of doing things? And how much of my spiritual journey is simply Beth's version of God's way?

Both of these thoughts lead me to a realization that I can only truly choose God's way when a) I am learning enough about God through His word to even know what God's way would look like, and b) I would only want to choose God's way over mine when I am walking with Him closely enough to remember constantly that His love and plan for me are bigger and better than my love and plan for myself.

Personal Touch

Spend some time reading in one of the gospels today. Make the effort to discover something about the character of God today through studying the life of Jesus. What was He really like? What would Jesus really have done in a given situation? We'll only know and be able to emulate His life when we truly become knowledgeable about Him...and we learn to fall in love with Him...either again or maybe even for the first time.

Prayer

Dear God, I must admit that sometimes it hits me how small You are in my mind, and how little I really know about Your character. Reveal Yourself to me as I draw near to You. Amen.

8

The Day that Changed All Our Lives

*Do you know how God controls the clouds
And makes His lightning flash?
Job 37:15*

I'd never felt that way before. For the first time in my life, I felt unsafe. Maybe I'd lived naively the past 30-plus years. Or maybe I'd never felt such threat before. I'm sure I wasn't the only one who was feeling this numb, what-do-we-do-now feeling.

But as a mother of two small children, that day, I couldn't help but hold them and kiss them and whisper to them over and over again that I loved them. I possibly lost a bit of the nonchalant bounce in my step. I know I will never mother the same again. I am forever changed. And I suspect

I am not the only one.

But I reminded myself of something – and I continue to remind myself in the days that have followed. This is not glib – this is not flippant – this is truth, whether we believe it in our gut or not, it is the truth: God is in control. And I believe that from my core…I had to or I wouldn't have been able to go on.

The God that I love and have given my life to – for whatever reason – allowed all of this. But that same God is all-knowing and all-powerful and ever-present and fully just and completely loving. And moms, He is getting us through this. The bounce in our step will come back – maybe not to the same degree, but if we lean into His care, it will come back. And our naiveté may be forever shaded – but the lessons we took away from all of this – how much bigger life is than our petty differences; how much larger a scheme of things there is compared to our tiny problems and inconveniences; that people – the people we love – are so much more important than our selfishness; and that, yes, we have a God who will walk us through this…those are lessons that will fill the void our lost innocence has left. And I remind myself of those lessons. I remind myself when the days are long and the arguments are plenty and the annoyances are petty…I remind myself that I am alive and that I am loved and that I have a job to do.

Moms – love your children, love your husbands, love your God. What else do we have, really?

Personal Touch

I'm sure you remember that day a bit like I did – it is a blur of emotions, but yet the memory of the planes tunneling into the World Trade Center has possibly been burned into all of our minds – and hearts. No matter how long ago this happened from when you're reading, please take a moment to pray for those who lost family members and friends that day.

Prayer

Dear God, we have no doubt that You are in control, but yet we still may be struggling with the why behind something as apparently senseless as thousands of people being killed at the hands of terrorists. Please help us remember that You could have stopped it from happening. My wise pastor reminded me that all You would have had to do was remove the gift of free will from the men who made those fatal decisions. However, to do so, You would have had to remove my free will as well. And with that gift, I freely choose to love You. Amen.

9

Busy *was* My Middle Name

There is a time for everything,
and a season for every activity under heaven.
Ecclesiastes 3:1

I used to pride myself on being an activity-aholic. Busy was my middle name. I thrived on it. I bragged about it. I reveled in it. I even complained about the pace...with a twinkle in my eye.

But then something happened awhile ago. I was looking at my schedule...with an activity (or two) marked in each day of the week as far as my eye could see. And I realized that I didn't want to live that kind of life anymore. So as the school year approached, I heard myself saying that one little word that packs so much punch, that carries so much weight, that I had almost never heard myself say...'no'. And I started weeding out my schedule, until I found myself at home with my children three to four full days each week.

At first, I thought for sure I would go stir crazy – just me and two little ones. Surely the white van would be coming down my street at any moment to take me away. But that is not at all what happened. My pace slowed. My mind cleared. My soul breathed a sigh of relief. And I began to enjoy life and see life and feel life. Stress lifted away. I began to know my children more deeply. I began to get to know myself again. And I began to notice God in the dailyness of my life.

One year later, I began preparing for another fall. And I found myself reaching back for last year's unhurried movements with longing. Because I had gotten myself into a bit of a bind. I had more on my list of to do's for the next six months than I had done over the past two or three years combined. And frankly, I was a bit scared that I'd bitten off too much. And I was definitely overwhelmed. In a way that I hadn't been in years.

If I were to list off all I had going, well…first of all, I don't think you'd believe me. And secondly, I think all it would do would make me wallow in self-pity a bit longer. So I won't. I'll just share with you that I had so wanted to spend this coming year just hanging out with my children (as this is our last 'normal' year together, before my Sara enters kindergarten next fall). But that was not going to happen. I had taken on projects – months-long projects – one huge one after another. And I was buried under regret, let alone wonderment as to how I planned to tackle all of this.

Are you feeling too busy? I have a theory. There are women who are too busy and know they are. Then there are women who are too busy and are in denial. Which one are you? I really believe that each woman can stand to shave at least one activity out of her life in an attempt to slow down and enjoy the really important things. What one activity (or two or three) do you think you can gently let go of for the sake of your sanity and your family?

Personal Touch

I was buried...but then I did something about it. In three steps. I listed all the relationships in my life that I felt called to pour into this year. And I listed all the roles that I had taken on. (I about fell out of my chair at this point!) So I prayed. Boy, did I pray! I felt hopeless as to what I could possibly say no to. Maybe because it was past saying no – I was going to have to undo some yes's. And because I am not a quitter, that seemed impossible to ask of myself. I took no actions – just spent about two days in prayer and thought about all of this. Then I did something huge. I quit! (Yikes!) I quit two huge tasks that I had just recently taken on. Both parties were so gracious and didn't make me feel badly for a second. And they understood my motives – they knew it wasn't a character issue with me, but that I had simply taken on more than I knew I could juggle well. Sweet relief. I have my life back for the next 9 months. I can write and I can head up the Women's Ministries at my church. But more importantly, I can build my home, spend unhurried time with my kids, love my husband, and rediscover God. Now this is the life I dreamed of. First of all, realistically determine your busyness level...ask your husband and a trusted friend what they think of your pace. And if you are in need of some priority rearranging, what steps can you take?

Prayer

Dear God, I'm too busy – I admit it. Please give me eyes to see exactly what I can let go of. Then not only give me the strength and wisdom to do so in a kind manner, but please bring someone forward to take my place. Amen.

10

The Brevity of This Life

Why, you do not even know what will happen tomorrow.
What is your life?
You are a mist that appears for a little while
and then vanishes.
James 4:14

I sit here before my computer screen just four days after learning of the death of a friend's husband. And I am compelled to write about it, but I am not so sure the words will come as easily as they usually do.

This is the closest I've been to the death experience. I lost my grandmother over 10 years ago, but that was different – she was a bit older, the next generation. This time, however – this man was 37 years old. He left behind a 36-year-old widow and three children, all under the age of 6. He was killed with a cliché that is not so much a cliché to me anymore – a car accident caused by a teenage drunk driver who survived.

I have so many random thoughts about this. How will she survive financially? Will she have to go to work? Did they have a good last night together? Will her children remember their daddy at all? Not only will she have to pick up with the details of life, but how much will she actually just miss his companionship? I don't think I realized until this moment – that though my husband, Kevin, and I have our fair share of struggles...who I am is completely wrapped up in being his wife and being partners in parenting with him. In the midst of a difficult time, I can flippantly let my mind wander that life could be so much easier if we just weren't together...but then something like this happens and jolts my little safe world back into gratitude and appreciation.

You know, I can wallow in self-pity parties all the time about how hard mothering can be. But who am I kidding now? How dare I think that thought ever again! My children have a father. I have a co-laborer in this effort who helps me get through. Ahh, but that's the point that I come back to again and again. Deb thought she did, too. I've been struck this week each time one of us has left the house and gotten in the car by the reality that that moment together could have been our last. We are not guaranteed anything in this life.

Well, at least we're not guaranteed anything that has to do with our humanity (except that we will each die at some point). But we are guaranteed something else. We all know that trouble is simply a part of being born; but that our Creator and our God has told us that He will never leave us. We can count on the fact that we are one prayer away from experiencing His complete peace. And yes, we are each potentially one breath away from our last.

What are you going to do with the moments that God has given you this day?

Personal Touch

It's easy to give lip service to the grand concept of stopping to smell the roses and all the other beautiful scents of life's mysteries – but what are you really going to do today to fully embrace your life?

Prayer

Dear God, It hits me time and again that life is really so short. Please remind me that my days have already been numbered – but that You are the holder of my life. Amen.

11

Women are Cool

Charm is deceptive, and beauty is fleeting;
But a woman who fears the Lord is to be praised.
Give her the reward she has earned,
And let her works bring her praise at the city gate.
Proverbs 31:30-31

I think women are absolutely incredible. I believe that God loves women and had a wonderful time creating each one of us. Once God made us and saw what He'd done, He was pleased...very pleased.

Just listen to all of the ways women were used by God throughout Scripture...the first miracle was at the request of Jesus' mother; the first declaration of Messiah-ship was to the woman at the well; Jesus actually spoke in public to Mary & Martha (which was huge back then); Mary Magdalene was the first to see Jesus after the resurrection;

and He chose to let her tell the disciples of the resurrection.

Also, I asked a few of my friends to give me some of their favorite reasons for being a girl and here's what they said:

- Having an excuse to change my mind as much as I want
- Being born with the incredible skill of multi-tasking
- Being able to discern and understand men better than they understand themselves
- Getting to participate in "girl talk"
- Men open doors and pick up heavy stuff for us (most of the time)
- I believe God has given females an extra sense of awareness and sensitivity to others: I like that and can use it to encourage others when they are in need.
- I like being part of the gender considered to be the more responsible and committed. In developing countries, groups giving small loans aiding poor families, only give to women. They have discovered from past experience, that women faithfully pay back their loans, men often do not. *Go girls!*
- I personally like not having the weight on my shoulders to "go out and earn a living" (though I think I'm "earning my keep" by being at home, no doubt!)
- I like being a girl so that I can do GIRLIE stuff. Like, arranging flowers and giving hugs to the people I love, even if we're in public, and trying to look pretty... BUT, being a tomboy if I wanna, too. Climbing hills and exploring streams, driving really fast around curves, and having spitting contests.

- And, my favorite reason of all…we are the privileged ones who get to give birth! Yay us! (Yes, ladies - it is a privilege!)

In processing all of this, I believe we should love *being* a woman. Do you? Do you sometimes struggle with seeing only your perceived limitations? Or can you catch a glimpse of the freedom that we have?

Personal Touch
Today I want you to celebrate your womanhood in a fun way. Call up your girlfriends and go for a daylong drive and go antiquing (if that's your thing). Kidnap your hubby for a lunch date. (Then allow him to open your doors!) Multi-task your little heart out – see how many goofy things you can do at the same time (chew gum, stir a pot of spaghetti, talk on the phone, quiet your toddler by throwing graham crackers at him, and paint your toenails) – then revel in your skills! Or change clothes 7 times in one day (and see if anyone notices). I was going to suggest giving birth – but I guess that's one you can't just do whenever you feel like it, now is it? You *can* have a spitting contest with your kids, though.

Prayer
Dear God, not that there is anything wrong at all with men – in fact, I know You made them and love them just as much as women – but thank You SO MUCH for making me a girl! I can't even imagine not being a woman and not being able to be as multi-faceted and emotional and full of possibility as I am. I love being a woman! Amen.

12

The Man You Share Your Life With

Her husband also {calls her blessed}, and he praises her:
'Many women do noble things, but you surpass them all.'
Proverbs 3:28b-29

If I were to ask you to picture your closest friend, does one particular person come to mind? Is it a girl??? I need to point out a lesson that I am currently working on...*your husband is your friend.* Some of you may be thinking, 'Duh? Of course he is...' But is he really? And if he is not, why not? Are you possibly the hindrance in the friendship? I read somewhere that you are your husband's best friend. Even if you can't picture that, look around his life – more than likely he is sharing more with you and depending more on you than he is anyone else. For him, you're it! What are you doing on your end to be his friend?

A girlfriend was sharing with me how she noticed that when she talks on the phone with her husband, she was matter-of-fact and curt, even showing disappointment in him. But that when she talked with her girlfriends on the phone, she was lighthearted and kind. That got me thinking, so I asked my husband a while back what I could do in our marriage for him to be more happy. His answer (that cut through my heart and pride), 'be nice to me'. Ouch. Why is it that we forget so quickly that the guy we married – you know, the one, as author Larry Crabb describes, that we eat with, sleep with, spend with, worship with, have kids with – is actually our friend?

Here's something I am currently working on — I have resolved to myself that I will share with Kevin first. I'm not just referring to stuff about Kevin or our marriage, but church stuff, friend stuff, things I'm struggling with. If I haven't shared it with Kevin, I won't share it with anyone else.

As far as specific marital problems go – please don't share these with all of your friends. Either seek out counseling if it's serious enough or if you just feel stuck, or find a woman you can trust who can mentor you in your marriage. Don't allow yourself to get together with your girlfriends and husband-bash. It really does no good.

So bottom line - ladies, we need to go to our husbands first. Your husband needs to be the most important person in your life. And I don't say this lightly - no matter the state of your marriage relationship. We are called to be wives before and long after our calling to mothering...so please make this a priority in your heart and with your time.

Personal Touch

Study your husband. What is his favorite meal? Make it. What meal does he hate? Stop making it ten times a month! What show does he like to watch on TV? Watch it with him.

What hobby does he have? Buy him a gift certificate towards it, then ask to help one day. And for heaven's sake – be nice to the man. It's really the least we can do.

Prayer

Dear God, thank You, really, for the man You allowed me to choose to be my husband. He has so many good qualities. Please open my eyes to them. Then open my mouth to thank You and him for them. Amen.

13

Takes Two to Tango?
Try Five

Though one can be overpowered,
two can defend themselves.
A cord of three strands is not quickly broken.
Ecclesiastes 4:12

There are five factors that are in play in your marriage that will determine its success or failure. You have an obstacle, an ally, an outsider, an enemy and an advocate.

When D.L. Moody was asked which group of people caused him the most grief over his pastoral career, he replied, "I've had more trouble with D.L. Moody than with any man alive." The obstacle, my dear, is you. You have the ability to trip yourself up at every turn, to miss chances to serve willingly, to jump at opportunities to get in the last word, and to speak in anger and without putting any thought into what comes out of your mouth. You are an obstacle. But you don't have to settle for that as fact. If Christ is your Forgiver and Leader, God wants to work on your heart to change you. Ask Him to show you the plank that is in your eye...ask Him to reveal to you where you're falling short...and my new favorite prayer – ask Him to guard your tongue. He will help you to remove yourself as an obstacle in the equation of your marriage.

You also have an ally...the man you married. Perhaps it has been a long while since you've thought of your husband as your partner or even simply as one of your friends. We must think back...unless a gun were involved, you chose your husband to be the man you wanted to spend the rest of your life with. You willingly chose him. Think back to why. Make a list if you have to...anything from, 'he goes to work every day to provide for us' to 'he plays with the kids' to 'last month, he brought me flowers'. Thank God for all the good things about him, asking Him to help you see him though His eyes. And ask God to simply strengthen your friendship. In the din of daily life – the mortgage, the kids, the laundry – we tend to forget about the friendship aspect. Enjoy your husband as your closest friend and ally in this long race called married life.

Then there is the outsider. These are people who don't uphold the value of marriage; who drag you down by husband-bashing as sport; who aren't in strong marriages themselves and secretly wish others could feel their pain. An outsider can also be another man who has qualities that you wish your spouse had...and you feel yourself developing feelings for. You must protect your marriage from outside sources that can bring harm to your relationship and even hurt your attitude toward marriage in general.

And you have an enemy...satan himself. Satan does not want your marriage to succeed. With every divorce, he celebrates. With every marriage that is mediocre, he is thrilled. It took me awhile to realize that Kevin was not my enemy, but that satan is. Just the other day, a young woman that I have spent time mentoring called me up to meet for lunch...she's getting married soon and she's having some jitters. That same morning, as I was packing up a few marriage books to loan her, Kevin and I were bickering like nobody's business...and as I'm stacking up those marriage books, I was muttering, 'How ironic! I have to go tell Lindsay that marriage is great when all I want to do is to tell her to run for the hills!' I have no doubt in my mind that satan wanted to undermine my confidence in my ability to encourage Lindsay about her upcoming marriage by making me feel like Kevin and I were doing far worse than we actually are. Thankfully, I recognized that and we patched things up before he left for the day...I wasn't going to let satan have even that small victory. He is our enemy and he is doing all he can to make our marriages difficult, with the intent to make them fail. Don't give him any ground.

But the best news – we have an advocate...Jesus Christ. He intercedes to the Father on our behalf. And He loves marriage. Marriage is to be a beautiful representation of the relationship between Christ and the Church, so of course, He is standing by willing to help us in any way we need to bring Him glory and to bring peace into our household. Lean on Him. Count on Him. Bring Him into your marriage in little, simple ways — pray for your marriage, for your husband, and for yourself as a wife. Ask that God will place a hedge of protection around your relationship. Ask Him to help both of you make your relationship your number one priority, after, of course, your relationship with Him. Pray with your husband. This is Marriage 401 here — something I think Kevin and I have only done maybe ten times in our marriage, but when we have, man, what a difference it has made — before sitting down to resolve a heavy conflict, stop and pray together asking the Spirit to help you both have softened hearts and help to work it out.

Personal Touch

There's more than just you and your husband in your marriage equation. But you can pray to be less of an obstacle, you can pray for your alliance to be strengthened, you can pray for protection from outside influences, you can pray that your enemy will not be able to successfully interfere, and you can pray that your Advocate join you as the third, and most integral, party in your relationship. After all, He created the concept — He will move heaven and earth to help you heal and succeed and love as He loves you.

Prayer

Dear God, Please move into the center of my marriage. Please protect our oneness and remind us of our vows daily, especially in the hard times. I am counting on You to help me have a strong marriage. Amen.

14

Friendships are a Worthy Investment

My intercessor is my friend as my eyes pour
out tears to God.
Job 16:20

"The rule of the universe," wrote C.S. Lewis to his friend, is "that others can do for us what we cannot do for ourselves, and one can paddle every canoe except one's own". For me, cultivating my friendships is a necessity – and it should be for you as well.

I read in a magazine article that the divorce rate is high partly because women are isolated from each other. It mentioned that so many of the things a healthy marriage needs, such as accountability, emotional support, and prayer flow from women's friendships.

Having girlfriends just seems to happen naturally for so many of us women, so I want to talk about the next level...some friendship lessons I've gleaned over the years.

Okay, let me touch briefly on relational conflict. This can be so tough. There's enough hard stuff in life to not have things going right with your girlfriends. But let me give you just a couple guidelines in this. First of all, if it's not a huge deal, seriously consider just prayerfully letting it go. However, if it is something that you really feel needs to be worked out, principle number one, don't go to anyone except the person involved. No one else needs to know the details. It dishonors the friendship to discuss the issue with others. Secondly, pray about it – that God will soften your heart and your friend's heart; as well as giving you the words to say. Then, take the initiative to bring restoration...whether you have been the victim or the offender, you should go to the person and extend a sincere apology for your part in the situation, then talk through it the best you can.

A silly example – one day, I was sitting on my porch and a girlfriend of mine who lives down the street went jogging by. As she was approaching, I was thinking all these encouraging thoughts like, 'That is so great! I am so proud of her! Keep up the good work!'. But I'm a sarcastic sinner so sometimes what is in my heart doesn't make it to my mouth and instead I yelled, "You make me sick!" as she passed. Now, she knows I'm ridiculously sarcastic, so she just smiled and waved; but immediately, I felt sick to my stomach. What just happened there?! I was thinking such nice things! I rushed to my computer and sent her an email apologizing...and telling her all the nice things I had actually been thinking. She wrote me back later that day saying that she knew the moment I said it that I would be mad at myself and she of course forgave me and knew that I meant it as encouragement. I could have let that go – but our friendship was too important for me to let harsh words just hang in the air, so I took the risk to be vulnerable and make it right. If you find yourself at odds with someone you really care about, take the initiative. It will be hard, no doubt, but so worth it.

Another guideline…guard your heart. That may seem like an odd thing to toss into the middle of a discussion on building friendship, but let me explain. A ways back, my trust was betrayed. Someone shared something that I had shared in confidence. I was devastated. But I learned an important lesson – not everyone in your life needs to know everything about your life. Choose wisely whom you will divulge the secrets of your soul. Make sure you're on the same page – a philosophy that I hold to (and now make sure that my closest friends hold to) is 'what is shared in this room stays in this room'. I can say anything with my closest girlfriends because I have taken the time to build relationships with women I can fully trust. Again, it is hard work. This won't come naturally. But I can walk with my head held high into a room knowing that the things I have shared in confidence with a select few have not been leaked to the masses.

And finally…let yourself be taken care of. Women are master caretakers. We are fabulous at jumping in at the first sign of a crisis and helping someone else. We are wonderful at writing encouragement notes or praying for our friends. But if we are about to go under…what do we do? If you're anything like me, you retreat. The little bad things – now those I share. The big bad things…for some reason, I get the idea in my head that I don't want to burden my friends as they have lives too. So I usually hunker down. But I have learned recently that there is a humility in letting someone in. It is a learned skill in being vulnerable enough to say 'help' or 'I can't seem to get through this on my own'. I've recently been gently taken care of through a hard situation…I am seriously a better person for it. You'll have to drop the defenses and be really honest, but that is an investment worthy of your finest efforts.

Personal Touch

How are your friendships doing? Do you have many, but they're shallow? Do you have too few to count on? Is your support system at the level you'd like it to be? Think of one thing you can do this week to strengthen that support.

Prayer

Dear God, help me to have the friendships that You want me to have...by being the friend that You want me to be. Amen.

15

The One That Really Can Meet All of Our Needs

For the king trusts in the Lord,
through the unfailing love of the Most High,
he will not be shaken.
Psalm 21:7

Several events lately have shaken me to my core. And those incidents have provided me with a new sense of urgency about sharing the most important thing in my life. Life is fragile and quick and we are each potentially one breath away from our last.

First and foremost, and I cannot keep writing without bringing this up – *do you have a personal relationship with Jesus?* Let me clarify what I mean by that. I am not asking if you attend church regularly. I am not asking if you have been confirmed. I am not asking if you consider yourself religious. I am not asking how much money you give to charity. I am not asking if your parents are religious, or if your husband is religious. In fact, I am not talking about religion at all.

I am talking about a personal relationship with Jesus as your personal Forgiver and Leader. Have you realized and acknowledged your own sin before our holy God? Do you truly believe that Jesus died on the cross *for you because you are a sinner*? Have you surrendered your life to Him, realizing that salvation is based upon nothing but grace and accepting His gift? There will be a day when you will stand before God – the Bible says that is the case – and it is truth whether you believe it or not – and He will want to know what you did with His Son and this life that He gave you.

So let me ask you – if you strip away all the duties and sometimes, all the burdens, that can sometimes come with 'being religious' – do you find a relationship with Jesus underneath it all? Can you point to a time in your life when you can clearly recall asking Jesus into your heart, asking for forgiveness of your personal sins, and proclaiming that you wanted to follow Him forever?

If so, fantastic – you are a follower of Christ.

If not, I would urge you to take the time to investigate the life of Jesus and His promises for you. This is a matter of life and death – of the eternal kind.

Okay, with all that said – I believe that God wants to be the Calm in the middle of my chaos…and in the middle of yours as well.

So we can agree that life is not always a piece of cake. Things get thrown at us that we're not expecting. Our circumstances, even if 'chosen' by us, leave us sometimes wanting. We married someone we love, but marriage is hard no matter how great the two people are. We wanted kids – but no one ever told us how daily and tiring being a mom can really be. God never said life would be easy or fair – but He said He would walk through it with us, if only we ask. He wants to be the Calm of each one of our lives.

But the key in all of this – is that you must ask Him to participate in your life…He will not enter uninvited…He is too kind and gracious to do that. So if you want His help and strength and wisdom, you must ask Him for it.

If I could, I would stand in front of you, dear reader, look you straight in the eye, call you by name and remind you: dear woman, wife, mother, and creation of God – if you remember nothing else from these writings, know this: you are loved by God. Intimately. Completely. Outrageously. Perfectly. Never ever forget that.

Personal Touch

Get out a blank piece of paper and write the following phrases (over and over again if you're so inclined):

> For God so loved me, that He gave His one and only Son that if I believe in Him I shall not perish but have eternal life.
> I am precious in His sight.
> This is love: not that I loved God, but that He loved me and sent His son as a sacrifice for my sins.
> God loves me.
> God loves me.
> God loves me.
> Intimately.
> Completely.
> Outrageously.
> Perfectly.
> I never want to forget that.

Prayer

Dear God, I think I finally get it. It's not just knowing

about You. I need to accept the gift that You paid a price for something that I could not repay on my own. I am a sinner. And You died for me! Please enter my heart, remove my sin, begin to make me new, and take over as Leader and Forgiver of my life. And remind me, remind me, remind me…over and over again…any way that You have to…that YOU LOVE ME. I can't get over it. You love me. Let me thank You with my life. Amen.

16

Catches My Eye

*No temptation has seized you except what
is common to man.
And God is faithful; He will not let you be tempted
beyond what you can bear.
But when you are tempted, He will also provide a way out
so that you can stand up under it.
I Corinthians 10:13*

Oh, my precious Sara. A girly girl through and through.
Last year she went through a bit of a phase of wearing
a leotard (fully loaded with tutu and crown and scepter, I
might add) around the house just for kicks. Like, every day,
basically. I thought it was cute, until I tried to take her out in
public and she refused to put on anything else.

Well, now, her preference is a dress. Every day. Even if
we're just hanging out at home. So in my attempt to appease

my daughter's boycott on pants, I have done my best to stock up on all kinds of dresses. Ones she can just kick around in at home, some for school, and some for church. Now, I also stumbled upon about 3 really wonderful dresses that I am saving for the holidays – these beauties will be perfect for Thanksgiving, Christmas and New Year's and all the festivities in between.

Here's the thing. A ways back, when tackling the clothing switch project (removing all summer clothes from her closet and replacing them with fall & winter), I filled her closet with all of her new dresses...including those sparkly, furry, dressy dresses set apart just for the holidays.

Well, you can just imagine her first glimpse into that closet – it was like a brand new wardrobe. So many choices (so many decisions!) – she now had a reason to change her outfit two and three and four times a day! (Oy vay!) But with as much flair as any human can muster, with that same human nature always looking for something they can't have – she asked to wear, each day, her Christmas dresses. And each day, for about three weeks, I told her the same thing, "No, honey – we're saving those for special occasions." And each day she'd pitch a mini fit and we'd have it out.

Until one day this week. She was deciding what to wear and proclaimed to me, pointing to those exceptional dresses, "But not these, right, Mommy? These are for special times, right?" And before I could say yes, she went on to say, in more wisdom than I usually have, "Mommy, can you just put them away then? I don't even want to see them anymore."

The temptation was too much for my precious little girl's heart to bear. She so much wanted to look her most beautiful, but her Mommy knew that if she wore them now, they wouldn't be as special later. And she just couldn't stand being told no anymore. So she asked to have them removed from her life until they could actually be choices in the running again. In fact, a few months later, she and I were taking a walk and we kept crossing paths with the ice cream man...and after I had told her that I didn't have any money so we wouldn't be getting any ice cream, she said, "Mommy, I am trying to not think about it but it keeps staying in my head... Maybe if you tell me a joke?"

Wow – how I wish I had the wisdom to take a look around my life and see what catches my eye that maybe shouldn't. Is there a person or thing or idea that steals a bit of my heart each day that I know I can't and shouldn't be even mulling over? I need to take matters into my own hands and remove the enticement from my life, or even have the maturity to distract myself when the object of my desire seems to keep just hanging around. Now that's wisdom.

Personal Touch

Maybe we'll just have to do that. Because our God, who occasionally says no to us, knows what He's talking about too. But how much easier on our hearts to not even have something in front of us that makes us drift in the first place. What catches your eye and heart that you know shouldn't? Is it junk food? Then don't buy snacks – if they're not in your home, you will not eat them. Is it spending money? Then limit the times you hit Target each month, only go when you have a list, and only buy what is on your list. Is it a feeling of envy when you see someone else's bigger home or better car? Spend some time in prayer this week simply thanking God for the tangible gifts He has given you and I guarantee your envy will fade with time.

Prayer

Dear God, please give me a sense of what trips me up in this life. Help me to know myself well. Then please give me the strength, wisdom and discipline to take steps to remove those barriers. The less temptation I place myself in, the less I will fall. Amen.

17

Smarter Than We Know

*And He said: 'Unless you change and
become like little children...''*
Matthew 18:3

When my daughter turned five, I feared the gimmies
would begin as she tends to want everything she sees
(wonder where she picked that up?!). But something
bizarre, yet quite nice, happened instead.

Somewhere along the line, literally 5 or 6 months before
her birthday, every time we were in any kind of store, she
would see something she liked and would ask if that item
could be on her birthday list. Where she got this concept, I
have no idea. At first, I doubted it would stick. But then I
noticed that each trip to the store would bring a peaceful
shopping venture with a few requests of birthday list addi-
tions. I could handle this!

One day, however, after she asked to add a bag of rice to her precious list, I pointed out that that list of hers was sure getting pretty long (and three months to go until the beloved day) and maybe we should put it to paper when we got home. Her response jolted me a bit – "No, Mommy, we don't need to write it down…"…tapping her finger against her head, she continued…"I've got it *all* right here."

Okay – yikes! I was so banking on the fact that once she left the store each time, everything she had just asked for was magically falling off the imaginary list. But now she was assuring me that it was all taken care of. Oh grand!

All this to say – our kids are not only smarter than we give them credit for, they may even be smarter than us from time to time. So step back and see what you can learn from them.

Personal Touch

Have you recently noticed something pretty 'deep' that has come from your child? First of all, write it down – you will forget it if you don't, and you'll be so glad to have this season of their lives chronicled. Then think about what they said – sometimes, God uses our kids and the situations they get themselves (and us!) in to teach us something. What can you glean from your child today?

Prayer

Dear God, sometimes my child says something that is so profound! Help me remember those times so I may cherish them in my heart. Then help me be open to any lesson You want me to learn from them. Amen.

18

Our Natural Bent

When the woman saw the fruit...she took some and ate it.
She also gave some to her husband...
Genesis 3:6a,c

Jack surprised me the other day. We were walking downstairs, he behind me. He was in a good mood, talking
about going on the computer, very happy. Then he muttered
the following phrase (and pardon my French, as my grandmother would say, in advance), "Stinky poopy."

Now, I had no idea what he was referring to – and
frankly, I didn't care. I turned around instantly and asked,
"What did you say?" (As he knows very clearly the rule in
our house – 'Corcorans' don't use words like that – we can
use better words'.) Here is where the surprise came – his
response: instantaneously, he said, "Nothing". You know
that 'nothing' – shifty eyes so as not to make contact with

mine, said very quickly, hands in the pocket. That is the kind of 'nothing' I would have expected from a 7 or 8 year old maybe – but from my baby?

He lied to me. My son chose to lie to me. He had the choice to come clean – but didn't. My son willingly chose sin.

Okay, I may sound a bit harsh here. Is it really sin if it's just a little white lie and no one got hurt? You better believe it is. It's sin when my young child does it, my precious son who can do no wrong (so I thought) and it's sin when I do it.

This just reminded me what I forget so very often. Just as Jack was a sinner since birth, sin engulfed my soul from infancy as well...just as it did for you. Scary, but true. Sad, but true. Unbelievable, but true... whether we believe it or not. Sin is our natural bent. Human beings are not innately good as most like to believe. We are depraved, with a capacity for good moments now and then.

So do whatever you can to slow the downward spiral of your child's sin nature. And while you're at it – prayerfully and diligently work as hard as you can at reversing your own downward spiral.

Personal Touch

Recognize and name your personal weakest area. Now make a workable, feasible plan for reducing this area of sin in your life.

Prayer

Dear God, I acknowledge my daily sin against You – my tendency to turn from You at every chance; and my specific daily sins – the choices I make that lead me farther away from You and Your plan for my life. I do not want sin to be my natural bent. Please overturn the effects of the curse in my life and make me holy. Amen.

19

Don't Forget – I'm Beautiful

*I praise you because I am fearfully a
nd wonderfully made.*
Psalm 139:14a

I was tucking Sara into bed the other night and we were praying. I asked if she wanted to pray or if she wanted me to pray. She pointed to me so I proceeded. I began thanking Jesus for making Sara my daughter, for making her so sweet, and so smart, and so strong and healthy, so funny, so gentle...then Sara stopped me and said, "Don't forget – I'm beautiful." So I continued, "And, of course, thank You for making Sara so beautiful."

Don't you wish we could have that same freedom and innocence? That lack of self-consciousness to say to ourselves and to those around us, 'don't forget – I'm beautiful'. And I don't mean just physical beauty. Though, how amazing if every woman truly felt the impressions of God's hand on her as His creation. But inner beauty. Being able to see how preciously we were each created from the inside out. Being able to see His hand on our lives and our character. Being able to be grateful for the little quirks and hangups that set us apart and make us unique.

That is what God wants for us. Just think about it. One of the greatest commandments is to love our neighbor as we love ourselves. Well, how can we love someone else well if we can barely stand who we've turned out to be? We need to come to a place of true acceptance. Even, yes, liking ourselves. It is not only okay to say – 'I like me' – it is what God wants for us. Afterall, He made us. And He said Himself that He is very pleased with what He's done.

Personal Touch

Read Psalm 139. After reading it, plug in your name where appropriate and write it out. Heck, frame it if you feel so led.

Prayer

Dear God, my mind knows You created me, but I just look at myself and how often I mess up and my heart sometimes forgets. Please remind me that I'm beautiful and precious to You...please help me not forget that I am a creation of the Master of the universe. Amen.

20

Refine Me

I am the Lord your God; consecrate yourselves
and be holy, because I am holy.
Leviticus 11:44

I was praying for my children this morning. Okay, in
truth, I was praying for my mothering. I've been doing
that a bit more lately. Lately I've been asking God to come
into my mothering in a deeper way, to make my mothering
holy. And today I heard myself pray that God refine me, not
just for Sara and Jack's sake, but for 'Your Kingdom'. It
seemed stronger than I'm used to phrasing it, but I kept
going. And here is my journal entry:

"If I am to bring Sara and Jack into a saving knowledge
of You (and that *is* what I want), and to influence them so
deeply, that when they are older, they fall in love with You
and bring others to You through their lives, *my mothering*

has to change. The inconsistencies, the yelling, the impatience – all of this must go! I want Sara and Jack with me in heaven and I want their mansions to be bigger and their crowns more precious than mine. Please, please refine me."

Please don't misinterpret my request for change. I am not a horrible mother. But I think most women would say that about themselves. Am I a holy mother, though? That should be my question and only bar of standard. Holiness. There is no room for sin and selfishness in holiness. Yet, we are, indeed, sinful and selfish women. Holiness seems so illusive; almost held for women of much higher caliber than you and I. You know – for women who are older or wiser or married to someone of spiritual influence or well-known for their life of faith? But holiness does not single anyone out. Well actually – that is exactly what it does. It asks us if we dare come close enough to truly attempt to understand it – than it shows us Jesus. Holiness is very inclusive.

I overheard a conversation of sorts between Sara and Jack...it went something like this: Sara, in a sing-songy, taunting voice, teased Jack, over and over again, "You are holy, you are holy, you are holy." To which he replied, angrily, "I am not!" Holding back a bit of laughter, I tried to console him that holy was the highest compliment he could ever hope to receive either side of heaven. He rebuffed me and they moved on in their discussion. (I didn't feel the theological need to correct her and tell her that Jack is sometimes the farthest thing from holy...) Because then I would have had to admit that I am even farther.

He is far from holy because he has a child's understanding of holy. I am far from holy and I somewhat (sometimes) get it. Which one of us is the farther removed?

Personal Touch

Take a look in your concordance and check out the long list of references to the words 'holy' and 'holiness'. Spend some time today reading several verses, writing down your thoughts about them, and praying for a deeper understanding of and desire for holiness to pervade your life.

Prayer

Dear God, You are holy. I can barely wrap my mind around that concept of perfection, of sinlessness. But You are. And You have so clearly called me to a life marked by holy thoughts, words and actions. Please open my eyes more clearly to Your truth, then refine me, one step at a time. Amen.

21

That Way!

In his heart a man plans his course,
but the Lord determines his steps.
Proverbs 16:9

Jack has come into his own lately. As I type that, I'm not smiling wistfully...I notice I have a huge crease in my forehead. *His own* seems to be something out of a horror movie. What used to be my laid-back mini-version of my husband – is now – well, not so laid back. He knows what he wants, when he wants it. And he'll let me know each and every want...for endless minutes at a time. Here's an example...the other day, he and I were in the van. I had an errand to run at a certain store and I needed to turn left. Jack wanted to go right. Since I am not a child-centered mom who thinks every whim of their child needs to be addressed and met, I kept going to my original destination. For 10 minutes, and I am not exaggerating to make this a better story, he repeated this phrase, "I want to go that way!", at the top of his lungs – sometimes intermingled with, "I want to go over there!" Normally, and I'll be really honest here, I tend to freak. That much screaming and for that amount of time just doesn't sit well with me and I start yelling right back at him. Sometimes as I sense my loopiness kicking in, I begin yelling – but not at him…I may just repeat what he's saying, but try to say it even more loudly that he is (with the philosophy of 'if you can't beat, join 'em'…). But this day, I had a different reaction. I stayed calm. And I said, firmly and loudly enough for him to hear me, "I love you, Jack!" That didn't stop him – but it stopped me. It stopped me from just being mad at him; from just thinking I must be a bad mother to have raised a child that yells at his parents for 10 minutes. And this is where my thoughts took me…

How often is my heart like Jack's toward my Parent? Though I may not pitch a fit (at least not on the outside) – if my heart is anytime less then fully yielded to what God is calling me to do, I am in disobedience. Was Jack being disobedient? Well, he didn't get out of his carseat, open the van door and begin walking 'that way'. He was simply voicing his opinion. Everyone is allowed to speak their minds – kids included. Really? Do you really believe that? I believe Jack could have said to me, 'I want to go that way." And I could have responded, 'we can't today, honey, I need to run to the store." And it should have been left at that. But he didn't just leave it. His reaction to me showed where his heart was (and I'm afraid to say, is, a lot of the time these days). His heart was not in line with pleasing his mommy. He cared about only one thing – himself. When I choose to put God off; when I choose to let Him know exactly what I want, thank you very much; when I choose to intentionally not heed His direction, I am being disobedient.

Now back to my 'I love you, Jack' response… How

often God must look upon us, see us wriggle out of His arms, watch us run from Him as He points the best way to go, listens to us bemoan His caring instruction – and then gently, patiently says to us, despite how we relate to Him (or despite the fact that we might not relate to Him at all), "I love you." "I will love you if you listen to Me; I will love you if you don't; I love you." Oh for my soul to remember that very fact every moment of every day.

Personal Touch

During your next spiritual meltdown – where you're telling God a thing or two about your life...remind your heart that He is listening and that He is loving you all the way through the struggling against Him.

Prayer

Dear God, I know that I do not listen to You as well as I should. First of all, I barely make time to hear You in the first place. And then when I do, I hold onto my plans with clenched fists, as if I really can come up with a better way for me to get through this little life of mine. I am sorry for not hearing, I am sorry for not listening, and I am sorry for not obeying. Thank You for forgiving me. Please remind my soul that You have my best interests at heart. Amen.

22

When Miss Type A Enters Solitude – Part I

Be still and know that I am God.
Psalm 46:10

A good deal of the time, I run through life. Picture Fred Flintstone doing what he does to get his car started...how he runs so fast you can't even see his feet anymore... That's me. However, I am not always in high gear. I seem to have two other shifts...there is the contemplative side of me, and then there is the slothful aspect, which we don't need to touch on right now. It's not black and white for me. Because of my quieter side — or perhaps, *because* of my Type A tendencies, a while ago I could tell I was in need of some alone time with God. So I made plans to spend four days at a spiritual retreat center...just me and God.

How did I know I needed to get away? I think I was waiting for an extended amount of alone time to just fall into my lap. What was I thinking? I have a husband, two young children, a house to take care of, a part-time position at my church, not to mention my writing and speaking ministry. Days with nothing going on just don't happen for me. So I knew I had to plan it. It really started to hit me when I began noticing some character issues — either ones I hadn't noticed before or ones that were surfacing more frequently.

Here was my particular list:

- I need rest. I seem to say that I'm tired a lot.
- I am simply tolerating motherhood these days.
- I watch too much television.
- I have lost the desire to journal.
- My creative well has run dry.
- The other day at church, when Susan didn't pick up her baby from the nursery right after the service was over, and Joann asked me where the plates were, and Kim talked my ear off about something I don't even remember, and Scott didn't turn in his information to me on time — all in a matter of about ten minutes — why did I snap at each one of them? In other words, my fuse is unusually short and my compassion level unusually low.
- I seem to be saying I'm sorry a lot. Not because I'm growing in humility, but because I'm messing up more.

So, basically, just a few things to kick around.

Now, you might not have a list like mine...but here are two questions that author and pastor, John Ortberg, uses to gauge how his soul is doing that he was given by Dallas

Willard to consider...

- Am I more easily discouraged?
- Am I more easily irritated?

Now don't get me wrong. Every time you feel discouraged or irritated does not require hauling yourself off to a monastery. I believe firmly that Jesus is our 'ever-present Teacher', as Richard Foster calls Him. I know He could have worked with me on my big issue at home...and I know this because it didn't take four days for us to crack that case...it was within the first 15 minutes that He and I settled it. However, there are just some things that can't get through in the noise and rush of daily life. And for that, going away may become necessary.

I think all my issues probably could have fallen under one of those two categories that Ortberg mentions. So I scoured my schedule, and my husband's, and my kids', and booked four days at a spiritual retreat center close to my home. However, booking it was just the beginning.

Personal Touch

Take a spiritual and emotional inventory. Are you more easily discouraged these days? Are you more easily irritated? When was the last time you had a good laugh, enjoyed a lingering few moments with God, took a walk that allowed you to clear your head? If 'can't even remember' is your answer — you might want to seriously consider a retreat.

Prayer

Dear God, I am tired and impatient these days...more than normal it seems. If time alone with You is what I need, I'm going to need Your help to swing it. Please help me to clear my schedule, figure out childcare and financially afford it. I need this. *We* need this. Amen.

23

When Miss Type A Enters Solitude – Part II

Be still before the Lord and wait patiently for Him.
Psalm 37:7

Here's how my time of solitude unfolded. I arrived at 9am on Monday morning. Okay, 8:50 — I was really excited to get started. But my assigned nun/tour guide wasn't there yet. So I had to sit and wait for ten minutes. As I watched the clock, I was thinking, 'Woman, where are you?!? Don't you know I want to spend time with God?!?' I guess you could say I was a little on edge…case in point of why I was there to begin with. I needed to get away.

It's not just about getting away from the everyday… though kids and dishes and laundry and cleaning and cooking and work and the husband can all wear on a woman from time to time, even though they are all blessings...for me, though, this time was just as much about what I was choosing to live without for four days...no television, no shopping, no fast food, no email (which is *huge* for me — when my husband and I went on a Caribbean cruise for a week, I checked email each day from the ship! — in the freaking Caribbean!), and no magazines (oh, but speaking of magazines...when walking to breakfast that first morning, I saw the latest issue of People in the nun's lounge and I began plotting how I could grab it without being caught...) ...another case in point of why I needed to be there...my propensity to be more concerned with getting caught than committing one of the seven deadly sins, let alone while on a spiritual retreat!

Basically, I filled my time with quiet meals, quiet quiet times, a quiet hour of writing about a dozen notes, some quiet reading outside, a quiet spell of laying on my bed looking out the window, quietly working my way towards finishing my first full reading of the Bible (not in one sitting...unless you'll allow me to count two years as one really long sitting), quietly napping, quietly lingering in prayer, quietly watching a gaggle of geese find their breakfast, and walking very, very slowly. Which beckons the question — how do you go from silent, slow, choreless monastic life back into the daily grind? Very, very carefully.

I was concerned about re-entry. In a few short days, I had come to relish the silence and the whispering. My life is not a quiet one. I didn't want to head back home with a chip on my shoulder as if to say, 'I was created for quiet and you people are ruining it for me'. So I realized that I needed to prepare myself for going back. I did three simple things. One, I made sure my husband knew when I was coming home so the house could be somewhat picked up (this might not be a thing for you, but it's a thing for me)...I didn't want my quiet heart to go out the window because I felt I had to grumble and straighten up my first hour back. Two, I had spent some time reading about various spiritual disciplines, so I jotted down a plan for implementing a few of them in my life. Saying that you want to try something is one thing...committing to try it by setting a goal and scheduling it on your calendar is quite another. And three, right before I left, I asked God to prepare my heart for going home. He and I agreed that, although that time had been wonderful for us, that is not real life. Did something supernatural happen while I was away? Yes, absolutely. A healing came to pass that I had desperately needed. It was restorative renewal at its best. However, true transformation into Christlikeness happens in the day to day. And I was about to head right back in with both barrels. I needed the peaceful spirit that I had settled into to stick...and I asked God to help it do so.

But what if you really, really cannot get away? If you find that your schedule or circumstances absolutely do not allow for an extended period of solitude, there are a few things you can do. First of all, most people can carve two or so hours out of their month...and that is what I would suggest. Start slowly — schedule an appointment on your calendar, two-three hours, once a month, for six months. Secondly, begin arranging your life around the concepts of retreating...how can you fit them into your normal day? It's one thing to tarry for fifteen minutes watching dragonflies chase each other over the surface of a babbling brook and chock that up as worshipping the Creator of the universe when you've got four days with nothing to do and nowhere to go...it's quite another when all you've got is fifteen minutes total to commune with God. You need to simply talk to God about it — He knows your life — He knows that you can't just stop your day for three hours to watch nature, but if you ask Him, He will give you creative ideas to bring Him more into your daily life. Go for a walk. If you live in a quiet neighborhood, use that time to pray or just observe creation. If your neighborhood is busy, bring a walkman and a worship tape. Get up fifteen minutes before everyone else, grab a cup of coffee, and sit outside, watching the sunrise. During lunch, light a candle, and sit down with your Bible instead of eating over the sink like you usually do. Walk slower. Talk less. Listen more. Simply quiet your heart.

Personal Touch

So, have you scheduled your retreat yet? What are you waiting for?

Prayer

Dear God, my time alone with You is on the calendar — please meet me there. Please help this time to be a time of renewal, rest, and reconnection between us. I can't wait! Amen.

24

Sweet Reassurance

Whom have I in heaven but You?
And earth has nothing I desire besides You.
Psalm 73:25

So I had received a not-so-favorable review for my first book. Something about inappropriate assumptions and stereotypical generalizations, yada yada yada. And I'm sharing my thoughts and disappointment with Sara over lunch – I ask her, "Sara, do you think Mommy uses 'tired gender stereotypes' when I speak and write?" Not really expecting an answer from my then 4-year-old, she replies, "Yes." I decide to probe further as that was not the opinion I hoped to gain from one of my biggest fans, "Give me an example." She sighs a little sigh and says, "Mommy, Jesus loves you. Jesus just always loves you." And I smiled (knowing she has just realigned my entire perspective on this subject), give her a kiss, and say, "You're right. Thank you, sweetie. You're the best." (To which she replied, "I *am* the best.")

Have you ever had one of those moments when your child, your baby, blows you away with simple faith and a life lesson that reminds you of truth? I love when that happens. In this instance, I was mulling over the fact that some critic didn't think my work was Pulitzer Prize caliber...I wasn't thinking about the handful of e-mails I had gotten just that week telling me that my book was just the encouragement that was needed at just the right time. I wasn't thinking about the reality that I had even gotten my book published so someone out there must have liked it to begin with. Nor was I even thinking about just the simple fact that my Heavenly Father loves me, so basically I needn't worry what other people think about me.

Sweet reassurance – all from the depth of wisdom of a young child. *Become like children*...now I know why...

Personal Touch

Do all you can to attune your hearing when your children are speaking to you. First of all, children that feel legitimately heard are happier, more secure children. But secondly, you never know what little nugget of truth they may pass on...and what life lesson God may want to teach you through them.

Prayer

Dear God, thank You for speaking so clearly through my kids. Who'd have thought how much wisdom they can truly impart to me? Please make me more aware of what my children are saying to me...I don't want to miss a thing! Amen.

25

I Mess Up, Too

*If we confess our sins, He is faithful and just
to forgive us our sins...*
I John 1:9

S ara disobeyed me this morning. Big-time. This is not
abnormal, but for whatever reason, it really shook me
today. She refused to go to school. Once we got there. So
there was a scene. I was almost in tears. It wasn't pretty.
Then we got back in the van. And I lost it. I was really
screaming at her. Now, don't get me wrong – I didn't hit her
or anything. But it was one of those moments when I actually thought, 'okay, I understand how child abuse can
happen'. Ever feel that way?

We went right back home, my plan for the morning basically shot as she was still crying, and I sent her to her room.
I had to keep myself busy and I wouldn't allow myself to go

get her, because I was still seething. I think part of it was the embarrassment; part of it was my feeling that basically she won that little battle, making sure I knew that she was boss; and part of it was shock that I was having to deal with a temper tantrum at her age. I think I had gotten to the point of expecting more out of Sara than that. She and I disagree all the time, and she is even more stubborn than I, but to pull something like that in public, just to prove a point? That blew me away.

I had some time to cool off, some time to think. And a couple things surfaced for me. One, I realized that even after she and I talked it through and I had calmed down, I still felt a bit disconnected from her. Like I said, she and I have our fair share of sparring, on a regular basis. But this was different. For that very brief moment in time, I didn't *like* my daughter. I was deeply disappointed in her character. And it made me question my mothering.

This thought of disconnection led me to think back to on our way home…there was a beautiful song on the radio – it was talking about how we can only imagine what it will be like when we finally see Jesus. This song has touched me time and again prior to today, but for some reason, God's holiness and my unworthiness plunged into my heart and I started crying.

Because first of all, my freaking out on Sara was no better than Sara's freaking out on me. And because I realized how very far away, on my own, I truly am from God. Because I understood my propensity to take the low road in the heat of the moment. Because I was reminded of a struggle – okay, let's call it what it is – a sin that I am currently losing a battle with in my life. This situation and this song came together to bring to light what disconnection God must feel with me sometimes. How I can let Him down so much too.

But there is good news at the end of my bad day. The

good news is that our Heavenly Father is just that – *Heavenly*. He is not human. He is not of this world. Though His heart breaks when we go against His chosen, and well-laid-out, order of things – He doesn't stay disconnected from me for long. Because there is Christ. There will always be Christ. Now that I know Jesus, I don't have to imagine what unbroken relationship means with my God. I can know. And I do.

Personal Touch

Have you hurt someone lately that you need to make amends with? Have you hurt the heart of God lately? He is waiting. Why not take some time today to just spend some time in confession. I bet your spirit will feel so much lighter.

Prayer

Dear God, I am so thankful that You are so faithful to cleanse us when we let You down. I've done it again...the same old thing. I am sorry that I can't seem to shake this sin...can't seem to rise above where I am and take the high road that I know You want me to take. Thank You for your promised sweet forgiveness, and please help me the next time around when I'm faced with that same temptation. Amen.

26

I Wonder as I Wander

…and we take captive every thought to make it obedient to Christ.
II Corinthians 10:5b

So Sara says to me in the van, 'Mom, are you thinking what I'm thinking?' Don't you just love when your kids repeat grown-up phrases? Especially when you're pretty sure they don't know what they're actually saying. So I had to smile. And reply. And I said, 'I seriously doubt it, but what are you thinking, honey?' She then said, 'Nothing!' and burst into giggles.

Actually, unfortunately, she was pretty close. I had just about nothing on my mind. If I did, it was definitely nothing worth thinking in the first place. I think I was in one of those random thought patterns where your mind floats around topics like 'I need to change the sheets' to 'what am I going to wear for Easter?' to 'I need to pray for Sue' then back to something banal again like 'I would kill for some chocolate'. Please tell me I'm not the only one who seems to have little control over my inner world sometimes. Please tell me those thoughts parallel your thoughts…at least sometimes.

But how I wish I could have longer stretches where my mind is not unoccupied…or when it is not occupied with meaningless trivialities. Reminded me of II Corinthians 10:5b: …and we take captive every thought to make it obedient to Christ. I really believe that God cares about how I spend every minute of my time, and that includes my mind-wandering moments.

Though, it may be built into us as humans to wander from time to time – and maybe that's a good stress-reducing habit – I know I sure can use a little thought captivity now and then…where I actually stop myself in mid-thought and redirect its path to something of higher value…something that is true or noble or right or pure or lovely or admirable or excellent or praiseworthy…something that will allow me to tell Sara next time that I actually am not thinking the same nothing that she's thinking…for once.

Personal Touch

Next time you catch yourself in the mind-wandering-mode, try this (espcially if it's a not-so-healthy train of thought): actually tell yourself to stop thinking what you're thinking, apologize to God if necessary, and begin to think about the holiness of God, or the salvation Christ provided for us, or what just might await us in heaven…wash your mind in things that are excellent…and derail that negative thought train.

Prayer

Dear God, I am thinking something I shouldn't be and I am sorry. My mind really can get the better of me sometimes.

Please help me to think on the good things of life, the amazing things of God. Please help to transform my mind and renew my heart. Amen.

27

Faith Like a Child

"Whoever humbles {herself} like this little child is the greatest in the Kingdom of heaven."
Matthew 18:4

A couple more faith lessons out of the moment-to-moment lives of my Sara and Jack. Jack was upset with Sara and rightly so. They had been using the computer together, and I had told Sara that when the big hand was on the four, it would be Jack's turn. Well, as you can guess, the big hand went right on past that little four without Sara blinking an eye…but Jack sure noticed, and he was not happy. He apparently tried to rectify the situation on his own, but with little success. They were in the basement and I was on the 2nd floor – I could hear their escalating voices two stories away. So as I was making my way downstairs to attempt yet another peace treaty, Jack met me in the hall. He looked up at me, didn't say a word (which was unusual), simply placed his hand in mine and led me back to the basement. He knew he was right and he was bringing the law-creator with him to be his law-enforcer. And it worked. We walked down the stairs slowly, almost methodically, as if Jack were hoping to prove a point and give Sara some time to make good on her own. She didn't – until she saw me hand-in-hand with her little nemesis. Then she said, half-heartedly, "Sorry, Jack," and moved over to the spectator seat. He smiled at me, let go of my hand, and started playing. All was well again. His mediator (me) didn't even have to say a word to get the job done...just my presence held authority. And I think of us...when we're tired of fighting the good fight, we can walk up to Jesus, take his hand, and walk back into battle with our law-enforcer. Or better still – when we've done something to let God down, we can still come before Him, with our mediator reminding God that we are His now...that simply being with Him in His presence – that holds authority. That day, Jack reminded me of the gift we have in Christ as our intercessor, as the One who bought us now and well into the future.

Now onto Sara. She and Daddy were playing and wrestling, having innocent fun together. When all of the sudden, she accidentally really hurt her Daddy and he sort of belted out an "Ouch!". It must have scared her and she must have felt terribly, because she just burst into tears and clung to him and kept saying over and over, between her tears and gulps for air, "I'm sorry, Daddy...I'm so sorry...I didn't mean to hurt you." I was stunned by the depth of pain she felt – she was still reeling emotionally well after Kevin was over his small physical affliction. And I almost felt an envy for her...for her intensity of repentance. I thought to myself, 'when was the last time I went to God and just sobbed, telling Him how sorry I was for my sin, for hurting Him?' It had been too long. But she reminded me in that moment how I really should see myself and my sin, how deeply I really should express my sorrow to my Father... and how, as Kevin did with Sara, He will hug me right back and whisper over and over that He loves me and that it's all okay.

Personal Touch

Today, when you're playing with your child, look at him through different eyes. Try to see her as God sees her. Try to picture the world as your child does. Slow down. Kneel down. Really, really look at them.

Prayer

Dear God, I still sometimes cannot believe that I'm a mother. I just look into the eyes of my children and I'm swept away sometimes. I see the freckles and memorize their places. I notice the whirl of color in their eyes. The dimple in the left cheek. And I know that no one else knows them the way I do. Thank You for creating this kind of mother love. I am in awe. Amen.

28

Because She First Liked Me

We love because He first loved us.
I John 4:19

Sara has taken to creating her own little songs these days…simple, not too profound, but very Sara. They usually involve pointing out her beauty at the time…still no shred of self-esteem issues with my precious girl. Then today, out of the blue, we were sitting outside on a gorgeous spring day…she had just picked a few tulips and was skipping up the driveway, and she looks at me and starts singing the most foundational parenting lesson I've ever been faced with, and says, "I like my Mommy because …la la la…she always likes me…la la la…and now I like the whole world." Oh my word! Let's break that down. My daughter is telling me that she likes me, she loves me, because I like her…in fact, because I *always* like her. My love and affinity for her must come first, before she can not only learn to love me - but going onto her other little gem – that she now likes the whole world – what she sees and who she interacts with – because of my foundational love for her. Wow. Now, of course, once again, my daughter was not trying to endow me with a parenting lesson (okay, maybe she was!), but she sure did. My love for her will shape her – it *is* shaping her. It will shape her love for me, it will form her love for her father and brother, it will influence her love of herself, it will mold her choices of what friends she lets into her heart and how well she loves them, it will even affect the man she selects to marry and how well she decides to love him.

Okay, are you feeling the pressure – the weight of your daughter's and son's complete future riding on your shoulders right about now? I don't want to give you immediate relief – I want you to sit with this thought for a minute, just sort of ruminating in the implications of these statements. It is a burden. Being someone's mother is the largest responsibility anyone can be presented, hands down. And we do have infinite power, way more than I think we realize, in how our children turn out – in how well they feel loved and in how well they end up loving. This is a huge task.

Okay, relief time. But alas, ladies, we are not alone. We can love our children well and fully and completely because we are loved first. And loved well and fully and completely. By Someone who really knows how to love.

And on the flipside, we can love yet selfishly and rudely and only moderately at times because that same Someone who is loving us and helping us love, is also loving our children. We are not the only ones who are loving them and showing them how to love...but we are still responsible to do so, with His help.

Personal Touch

This week, work on telling your child you love them at

least once each day. But don't just tell them. Hold them while you tell them. And tell them *why* you love them.

Prayer

Dear God, I know that I can only love because You have loved me first. I know I don't have it in me. I do when things are going alright, but when it gets rough, when the kids start acting up, that 'natural' love sort of drains out of me. I need You to fill up my emotional well so I have more than enough to go around to the people in my life. Amen.

29

Buckle Up

It should be that of your inner self, the unfading beauty
of a gentle and quiet spirit,
which is of great worth in God's sight.
I Peter 3:4

I just saw a woman letting her young children sit in the
front seat of her car, not only not in carseats, but unbuck-
led as well. That gets under my skin so much. I was saying
out loud to myself, 'Citizen's arrest! Citizen's arrest!'

Then I felt the gentle nudging of the Holy Spirit – 'Beth,
don't be too judgmental…she may be being reckless with
her children physically…but are there any areas that you are
reckless with Sara and Jack emotionally or spiritually?'

Ouch. Maybe my kids are booster-seated-in every time
we hop in the van, but on a consistent basis, am I strapping
them in with my love? Do they know beyond a shadow of a

doubt at every turn that I love them completely? Do they feel appreciated enough to be themselves? Protected enough to try new things? Secure enough to leave the fold now and then?

Am I buckling them up in the love of God? Do they know – I mean really know - in their albeit limited, childlike capacity – that Jesus died for *them*, because He *loves them*? Are they hemmed in with the immensity of God? Are they fastened together with the knowledge that they were created by the Creator of all things?

Am I telling them all these things?

Am I showing them all these things?

Or am I just being reckless?

Personal Touch

Be very watchful of the recklessness of your words and actions…you are being watched. You are being studied. You are about to be imitated.

Prayer

Dear God, I need Your help to approach my children's hearts with gentleness and kindness. Forgive me for my past reckless behavior with Your creations. Please change me. Amen.

30

A Walk through the Desert

If I make my bed in the depths,
You are there.
Psalm 139:8b

I'm in a desert...a valley...a lowland. Call it what you will.

I'm tired of crying.

I'm tired of being sad.

I'm tired of yelling at Sara and Jack.

I'm tired of my Gramma dying.

I'm tired of sighing.

I'm tired of having little energy.

I'm tired of having little motivation.

I'm tired of having so little patience and not enough joy.

I'm tired of just barking at my kids.

I'm tired of waiting for my second book to be published

when in actuality I think I just need to let my dream go.

I'm tired of being a mother.

I'm tired of being tired of being a mother.

I'm tired of being bored.

I'm tired of being tired.

When do you just push through? When do you just grin and bear it? When do you make drastic changes? How do you know what to change when you've always done things the way you've done them?

I wrote the above a few months ago...I was this close to filling a prescription for anti-depressants. I knew something was wrong with me, but couldn't put my finger on it. Or at least, didn't want to. I was depressed in a way I hadn't been before. And I was so confused and frustrated. When I'd share with friends, I'd say things like, "I'm doing everything I always do (walk, take vitamins, have quiet times, get enough sleep, have time with friends, etc.)...so what's wrong with me?"

You know, I've come to realize that some deserts just come. That there are times in your life when, for whatever reason, the hand of God is nowhere to be found in your life (His hand is still there, we just can't always see it). Times when you feel lost in the midst of walking the walk as faithfully as you can. And then there are self-inflicted deserts... trips to the lowland that you brought on yourself. In hindsight, I know which mine was. For four months, I lived a life of unconfessed sin. I went to church. I mothered. I prayed. I was a wife. I fasted. I was a friend. I served. I wrote. I began reading the Bible all the way through for the first time. I spoke. I led. All under a heart covered over by a particular hidden sin. I don't begin to act as if I fully understand what all that means. Other than I believe that though the Spirit is with me at all times, has been and will always, ever since I accepted Christ when I was 15...I had quenched His work in my life. How much? I don't know. What earthly consequences were there?

I'm still wading through. What eternal damage did I do – or, what Kingdom work did I hinder? I won't know til quite a bit later. (Notice that the Bible doesn't say that there will be no crying in heaven? It says that Jesus will wipe away our tears...I think this will be one of my Savior-wiping-tears times...4 months of life basically lost...)

But I do know a couple things. Once I woke up to my sin-stained reality and got past the fact that confessing just to God, for me, wasn't going to be enough...and took my pride and smashed it on the floor by confiding in my husband and two of my closest friends...the depression evaporated. Satan no longer had a stronghold in my heart and life. I kicked him in the gut when I went public with my sin and shame. And another thing I know...I never, and I mean never, want to be a wife, mother, friend, servant, leader, writer, speaker and, most importantly, child of God without the Spirit's complete reign over my soul. I never again want to quell what He wants to do through me. I never again want to let Him down like that.

However, my life is richer now...I have a joy and a lightness to my step that I may not have had even before that fateful choice of mine all those months ago...because though I'd give anything to go back in time and choose the high road in that moment, I know, really, really know what grace is now. My husband modeled it to me as he held me and my friends exemplified it to me as they cried with me. And I have felt the smile of God on my life as He has helped me mend the wrongs I did. So if it took a desert to get me to the mountain of grace rediscovery, then so be it. Only next time, Lord, may it be a valley of Your doing, not by my own hand.

Personal Touch

In a desert of your own? Don't go through it alone. Pray about it. Share it with a friend. Journal through it.

On a bit of a high? Then store up now for the time when

you go through the valleys – because it's just a matter of time. Life is filled with ups and downs.

Prayer

Dear God, I don't hear You all that well right now. But I know that You are still there. Whether this time of sighing is self-imposed or circumstantial beyond my ability to change it, please meet me here and 'don't forget me forever'. Amen.

31

Of Death and Dying

Though I walk through the valley of the shadow of death,
I shall not fear.
Psalm 23:4

My Grampa opened the door of their nursing home suite. It was the first time I had seen them in two years, I had been warned not to have too high of expectations. I was expecting two shrunken, sick-looking versions of my grandparents, but that's not what I experienced at all. They both *looked* the same to me. My Gramma has been battling cancer on and off for a few years, and my Grampa had begun to exhibit symptoms of depression with their move from Florida to an Illinois care facility.

Here's what I wasn't expecting. I immediately leaned in to give a hug to my Grampa...this man who I love so dearly, who has been one of my biggest fans for as long as I can remember, who always makes me smile with a joke or kind word…and he whispered in my ear, "I'm not the same person anymore." It's one thing to not be the same person anymore. It's a whole different situation to not be same person anymore, but be aware of it enough to know you're not the same person…that just seems cruel to me. And I began to cry. And held onto him a bit longer than maybe I normally would. And I said, 'It's okay, Grampa,' even though I was pretty sure I didn't believe that, and I knew he didn't believe that.

And so began a few months of slow heartbreak for me. I went back to see them two other times in the months that followed. My Grampa's depression had taken hold and he didn't seem to be able to gain back any ground on his own. To the point that he was moved out of their suite.

And my Gramma…well, I simply saw up-close a person die slowly and painfully. That experience was one of the hardest things I've ever been through – because I love them both so much and completely despised to see them both hurting so much in their own ways. But it was also oddly sweet – as I had the boldness to remind them time and again at our visits and through letters how much I love them and of the perfect and complete love and peace of our God.

But I'm left sadly with an unformulated thought that I cannot shake…I've come to the conclusion that, though I'm only in my mid-thirties, death in and of itself does not scare me. I'm convinced enough of where I'm headed. What sucks though (and how I wish I could find a more mature word for it) – what sucks though is the dying. I'm not quite sure why my precious, frail Gramma has to suffer with cancer eating into her throat. I'm not quite sure why this woman who loves Jesus has the knowledge that her fate ends with either suffocation or bleeding to death from a radiation wound that won't heal. Life doesn't feel as sweet in light of my Gramma's drawn out misery. And I'm not placated with the answer of 'there is sin in the world'. That's not quite cutting it for me right now. Nor am I quite ready to ask God. Part of me doesn't want to know. I know where they are going. And I know where I am going. And I know that Jesus will walk us each through to the end...no matter how hard and bitter and treacherous it might be.

Personal Touch

How do you experience your times of loss? Do you rush through them because they're just too painful? May I suggest something slightly radical...the good comes from the same Hand that the bad in life comes from...maybe next time around, you can let yourself just live in it...let the pain linger...make sure you are fully processing it...for your sake and for the emotional legacy you are leaving for your children.

Prayer

Dear God, please remind me where I'm going. Please remind mc that You number my days and are holding me close. Amen.

32

The Timeout King

Train up a child in the way he should go,
and even when he is old he will not depart from it.
Proverbs 22:6

My son began preschool recently and he was so
excited. I was too...for him, for me, for the fun of
watching life unfold and move ahead. I believe it was on his
third day of school that his teacher walked out with him,
Jack's head hanging low, telling me that he 'didn't do very
well today' and that after three chances, he was placed in
timeout. Okay, now, I'm not one of those moms who blindly
think my kids walk on water, faultless and brilliant. I know
their limits. So, frankly, Jack not being able to focus for
three hours didn't come as a shock. Jack being the *first* child
to get a timeout for the year – well, that sort of rubbed me
the wrong way, stung a bit even. But I tried to shake it off,

thinking maybe he just had an off day. Well, two more time-outs later, (and only about two more class sessions later) I was frustrated. Not knowing why my son couldn't seem to handle this new situation. But not only that...I apparently am the mom who has raised the kid who causes the most trouble in his class. That's a feeling that creeps back into my mind throughout the day.

So, not only was I dealing with Jack – simply, what was I going to do to get him to behave? (He goes to kindergarten next year – sitting still and not talking out and not wrestling the other kids are all things he kind of needs to master in the next 9 months...) Taking all his privileges away (videos, computer time, outside time, story time even) – none of those things were working. I even specifically went to Burger King on a day he got a timeout, and asked as we entered the drive thru lane, 'Who listened to their teacher today?', then proceeded to order chicken nuggets for my *perfect* child, Sara, and not for Jack. Nothin'. He couldn't care less. So, what to do with him? And, sigh, what to do with me? Now that I've let my little one out into the world and found that seemingly he wasn't given the skills he was supposed to get...by me.

Now what? Well, thankfully, I brought my son and this situation to the only One who knows the answers – even to things like preschool timeout predicaments.

And within a week, I ran across a book, through several different channels, on raising boys. There was an answer to prayer on the practicals of what I could be doing.

And I came to a place of realizing that he just may not be ready, and I told God (much to my surprise) that if he needed to just be home another year, then pushing kinder-garten off for a year to try another whack at preschool next year, that would be what I would do, happily. Answer to prayer regarding my hurting, confused heart.

And then a call from the preschool director – which I

almost didn't answer on purpose! – 'Jack is academically advanced – he knows all these things already...maybe he just needs to be in the class that meets three days a week and is doing more kindergarten preparation work', she offered. 'Okay', I said (sending up a prayer of 'what a relief that would be to my heart if he were just bored this whole time' – and – 'wow, you answer fast, Lord!').

So Jack is going three days a week. We're a few classes into it – and his teacher said this has made all the difference.

Lessons learned: my son is not the worst kid in the world. I'm not the worst mother either. And – oh, yeh, God hears me...even on the little things...and responds... sweetly, gently, intimately.

Personal Touch

I tend to pray for something...forget I prayed for it... watch something cool happen in my life...forget that it is actually an answered prayer and not just a coincidence...and move on. Do you ever find yourself doing that? Forgetting what you prayed for? Forgetting to acknowledge God's hand in your circumstances? Try writing down your requests for a couple weeks and track how He moves in your life. Then make sure you thank Him for hearing you and responding.

Prayer

Dear God, may I be mindful and watchful of the answers to prayer sprinkled throughout my life. Thank You for answering me. Amen.

33

Who Me,
High Maintenance?

Charm is deceitful and beauty is vain,
but a woman who fears the LORD, she shall be praised.
Proverbs 31:30

I saw a beautiful woman today while I was dropping my
son off at preschool – a fellow mom…and in my sinful
envy, I muttered quietly under my breath, "Wow – high
maintenance." Now, please know that I caught myself
quickly enough to repent. Okay, actually, *I* didn't catch
myself. The Spirit did. I believe His words to me were, "As
are you, my dear." Ouch. Unfortunately, checking myself
out in my minivan window's reflection and catching a
glimpse of a baseball cap-clad, sweats-donning, very-much-
entrenched-in-her-30's (albeit early 30's!) mom, I knew the

Spirit was not referring to my physical appearance. Didn't take long to pull that look together. (Though, tangentially, sadly, probably longer than I'd like to admit!)

Ahhh, high maintenance. I was introduced to that phrase during my first viewing of "When Harry Met Sally". Do you remember that movie and that scene? Meg Ryan, I believe, was ordering lunch, with just about everything 'on the side'; and Billy Crystal made a comment about her being high maintenance. And that the worst kind of woman, is the one who is high maintenance, and yet doesn't know it and/or admit it. Meg's character, Sally, was livid and balked at his critique of her. Case in point.

I am the easy kind of high maintenance (if there is such a paradox!) - self-diagnosed, self-aware, self-deprecating. My poor, sweet husband. What a handful he has in me. Anyway, my point. My point is not to flaunt how difficult I am, or how much time I spend on my hair, or how I also find joy in ordering many, many things 'on the side'.

It's the Spirit's gentle voice pointing out that I am a handful to Him as well. He has to work overtime with me. Just in the fact that I momentarily and silently belittled another woman for being pretty...that tips me off to the state of my heart. I am sinful. He has his work cut out with me. But somehow, and this is the beauty and mystery of grace, He seems to not just *endure* me, but His word actually tells me that I am precious in His sight...I am summoned by my name...I am redeemed...and He loves me. Every difficult, sinful, high-maintenance ounce of me. And every difficult, sinful, high-maintenance ounce of you. Fully loved. Fully maintained.

Personal Touch

There is freedom in being aware of your own personality quirks. High maintenance? Cranky when deprived of a good night's sleep? Forgetful when stressed? Headachy when hungry? You know the little things about you that make you unique, but that also can make you somebody's handful. Try to catch those times beforehand...be ready for them...prepare others around you for them.

Prayer

Dear God, thank You for loving me as is. Why and how You do it is beyond me...but You do it nonetheless. Thank You for not just putting up with me, but for cherishing me and helping me become more like Your Son. Amen.

34

The Truth Hurts

Instead, speaking the truth in love, we will in
all things grow up into him
who is the Head, that is, Christ.
Ephesians 4:15

Another family moment within the confines of the minivan...minivan, sweet minivan. Sara and Jack were
being their normal kinda loud, kinda annoying selves, carrying on their normal kinda frustrating, kinda maddening
minivan behavior. They were arguing over a book or something...you know the kind of thing where that book has
been there for probably two months, but because one of
them was reading it, the other just had to have it right then
and there. So, I was doing my typical best to tune them out
with the radio (worship tunes of course!), or prayer, or some
type of mantra like, "I am not going crazy...I am not going

to lose my mind…this too shall pass…" When all of the sudden, Sara gives Jack the book and says to me, "Mommy – I want to ask you a question." 'Okay', I said, almost a little afraid. "Did you have two kids so that we would fight and leave you alone?" Before the words, "Oh, don't be silly… Mommy and Daddy had two kids because we wanted to have a family to love and take care of, blah blah blah", could come out of my mouth, I said, 'Pretty much.' And she said, "That's what I thought."

This was one of those times when seizing the teachable moment felt a little out of reach…my reserves were spent and I had nothing to give. Did I feel even the slightest bit guilty that I answered my sensitive and inquisitive daughter with sarcasm? Not really. What can I say – some days my head hits the pillow a little lighter than others…this was just not one of those days.

Personal Touch

Cut yourself some slack – not every moment in life must be a teachable moment. Not every word you say will be dripping with wisdom and grace. It's a goal, not a requirement worthy of guilt if you miss the mark.

Prayer

Dear God, help me to know what to say to my kids when they ask those tough questions. Help me not to pass on my sarcasm or negativity. But help me to show myself some grace when I mess up…after all, You do every time. Amen.

35

They Weren't the Only Ones Surprised

Do everything without complaining...
Philippians 2:14a

I planned a special treat for my kids ...I was taking them
to a movie – one that they both wanted to see - at an
actual movie theater. I woke them up and told them that we
had a couple errands and then I had a surprise for them. The
morning was peppered with guesses and their anticipation
was almost palpable...Sara and Jack were so excited. I took
them for a quick lunch then told them on the way to the
theater where we were going and what we were going to
see...they were thrilled. And I felt like I had scored some
huge Mommy points with my kids. So we went – we had a
great time – they were on the edge of their seats, enjoying

every moment of the movie. Then the lights came up.

No 'thank you, Mommy' left the lips of either of my kids. In fact, Sara even had the gall to say, "Can we go one more place before we go home, Mommy? *That wasn't a good enough surprise.*" I was immediately angered by their ingratitude, by their greed, by their lack of appreciation for the two hours I had just given up, not to mention the fifteen bucks. But those feelings were quickly pushed aside by sadness…sadness that I had raised children who lived so in the moment that they couldn't appreciate their most recent gifts. Sadness that they had almost already forgotten the fun they had just had, and that I was the one who had given it to them. And then just sadness…because that was not what I had expected or hoped would be the outcome of that gift.

Oh, but isn't this us? Ungrateful. Forgetful. The house that we just had to have, prayed for, even delighted in for awhile…now seems too small or outdated, simply lacking. The husband we couldn't imagine our lives without now sends us to the Throne Room saying, "Why did you let me marry this man, God??" The kids we longed for, hoped for…who of us hasn't said, "Being a mom is so hard, Lord – I can't handle this! I don't *want* to handle this!" Even the dream that was fulfilled – the dream that enlarged your faith in God…even that can become blurry with the deceptive hands of time, leaving you asking for a new dream, this time even bigger, 'so I can know that it really is from Your hand, God."

A friend of mine said something like, "Most of our complaints, our requests for help in prayer, are over blessings in our life, even things we asked for." The house (money pit!), the husband (why can't he meet my needs?), the kids (they drive me crazy!), the dream (one more time, God – the last one wasn't a good enough surprise!)…all things we asked for. All things we always wanted. Never good enough for the ungrateful…never recent enough for the forgetful.

I want to be a woman of gratitude. I want to be a remember-er of God's goodness and gifts in my life. I want the joy of the anticipation that comes out of a knowledge that the Giver in my life can be trusted, that He is actually grateful for me, and that He will never, ever forget who I am and that I am His.

Personal Touch
Anything you've been ungrateful over lately? Why don't you spend some time handing it over to God – tell Him you're sorry for the ingratitude, and tell Him you're thankful for that gift.

Prayer
Dear God, You have given me so many amazing things...family, friends, home, fulfilling work...I am sorry for the times I seem ungrateful. Please remind me that the gifts in my life come from You. Please give me a heart of gratitude. Thank You for Your love and Your blessings. Amen.

36

What's in a Name?

May your fountain be blessed, and may you rejoice in the {spouse} of your youth.
Proverbs 5:18

We're going to take a little tangent today, ladies. We're going to talk about the men in our lives. I don't know about you – but laughter is hugely important to me. I love to laugh…and my husband, Kevin, in his deadpan way, makes me laugh harder than anyone else can. (Probably one solid reason I married him…)

The other day, we were in the kitchen, kind of late in the day, and I had dropped a piece of paper on the floor. It was one of those things where I thought it had floated under the frig or something and I couldn't find it and, within about three seconds, I was saying things like, "Where did it go? How could I have lost it? Am I losing my mind?" And

Kevin was standing there having to hold back the laughter because it was, of course, right by my feet the entire time. Well, to save face, I claimed that I couldn't see it because 'it is like a cave in here!', I exclaimed adamantly. You see, my husband keeps the lights off as much as possible (it drives me crazy)...and I was trying to shift the blame from my goofiness onto him somehow, so I 'attacked' his frugality. To my cave comment, he said, 'You mean, it's wet in here? You hear bats?' He then said, 'Just turn the light on if it bugs you so much.' So I did, even though I was planning to leave the room. Then I said, "I'm just going to stand here so that you have to leave the light on." He said, "Do you hear what you're saying – what I have to put up with? You'd leave lights on all over the house all day long if you could. You turn lights on, then go for a walk! You're two streets away and I'm processing your need for ambience!" I was literally on the floor, doubled over, tears running down my face. (You've got to hear how he pronounces 'ambience'!)

Then the other day, I told Kevin that I wanted him to come up with a nickname for me. Something other than *honey* or *Beth*. Something that meant something to both of us. And something that was actually nice. I explained to him that two of our couple friends' husbands have nicknames for their wives and I thought it was really sweet. He sighed, rolled his eyes, and said, 'You're kidding me, right?' But he started throwing some out nevertheless.

'Toots?' *Um, no.*

'Slim?' *Why?* 'Because you're slim.' *Thank you, but no.*

'Winnie?' *Winnie?!* 'You say, 'I win' a lot.' *No I don't... so no.*

'Blackie?' *What?* 'You look good in black?', he said with a bit of a question, his weariness showing, his creativity waning. *Again, thank you, but no.*

'Peri?' *Why Peri?* 'Your favorite color is periwinkle.' *No...no it's not. I actually dislike periwinkle.* (By this time,

I'm beginning to wane...)

Til he tossed out his final offering, and quite confidently I must add, 'Seven.' *Seven? Are you kidding me? Why?* 'It's your favorite number.' *No it's not,* I said with a sigh of resignation. 'Well, what's your favorite number then?' *63.* '63?! Whose favorite number is 63?! And who *calls* anyone 63?!' *No one calls anyone by their favorite number! Ugh...never mind.*

Just a peek into our goofy life. And there's only one reason I gave you this private peek...because I want to encourage you to find the idiosyncrasies in your relationship that make it so unique, that remind you that your lives are so intertwined the bond is unbreakable, to remind you that you have a history and a present and a future...and to remind you that all of this is a gift from God.

Personal Touch

Laugh with your husband today. Do something fun with him. Set up a date. Do anything it takes to remind the two of you that although life is hard and serious, you are each other's friends and it is important that you enjoy each other's company.

Prayer

Dear God, thank You for my husband. Thank You for making us friends and making us one. Help us to be better friends to each other. Help us to lighten each other's loads and moods. Help us grow in this relationship. Amen.

37

Relationships 101

A wife of noble character who can find?
She is worth far more than rubies.
Her husband has full confidence in her and lacks
nothing of value.
She brings him good, not harm, all the days of her life.
Proverbs 31: 10-12

M y husband, Kevin, and I were having one of those days where disconnection was prevailing. We both were handling the situation poorly, but life has to go on and sometimes you can't fix something before he heads off to work or you have to run the kids to school. So we had a day or so on not-so-good terms. It was run-of-the-mill stuff, nothing huge. In fact, I don't even remember what started it. (Okay, well, I do…but that's not the point…)

So the kids and I were cuddling on the couch waiting for

Daddy to come home for dinner, and Jack snuggles close to me and says, "This is what Daddy's going to do when he gets home." It was very sweet. But I said, "Probably not today, honey…Daddy's a little upset with me." And Sara said, "Ah, Mom…", kind of like, 'what did you do now?' Just as we were talking, Kevin came home and the kids went running to greet him. I walked into the kitchen to get dinner on the table. He and I didn't really look at each other, let alone say anything, while he was greeting the kids. But Sara comes over to me, nudges me and says, reminiscent of two junior high girls at their first dance, "Mom, go to talk to him." Made me smile. And it worked – we made up that evening.

This incident really got to me – for a couple reasons. One, Jack was able to imitate the kind of affection Kevin shows me – because he's seen him do it. And secondly, Sara was visibly bothered by the knowledge that her Mommy and Daddy weren't okay. That didn't sit well with her. In fact, she wanted us to fix it. And she took matters into her own hands to get me to initiate communication. My children are watching. They are listening. They see how well (or not well) Kevin and I treat each other. They feel the distance… just as they can feel the genuine love. And we are showing them each what to expect out of marriage…which is really scary sometimes. Sara will make Kevin the standard from which she chooses her husband, and Jack will more than likely treat his wife the way he observes Kevin treat me. That goes the other way as well…Sara will love and respect her husband with what she sees me model, and Jack will choose a wife based on what he likes in me.

Personal Touch

Two points of challenge and encouragement today, ladies. Take extra care with your marriage – this is not just a relationship that affects you and your husband…it will have lasting effects on your children. Treat your husband's heart with gentleness, show him respect, display your affection for him openly. And secondly, pray, pray, pray for the spouse your child chooses…their choice will rest a lot on what they see in you and your husband; and it will affect their lifetime's contentment level, their children's lives, and their spiritual effectiveness.

Prayer

Dear God, help my marriage be a solid foundation for the choices of my children. Help them learn what it means to have a good marriage from watching their father and me. And please provide both of them with amazing spouses at just the right time in their lives. Amen.

38

There's More to Come

Behold, I will create new heavens and a new earth.
The former things will not be remembered,
nor will they come to mind.
Isaiah 65:17

A friend invited me to be a part of a pretty special occasion in the life of her family...the birth of her first son. I met up with them at the hospital and stuck around for the last 12 hours of her labor, through the actual birth. What an incredible experience. Part of me isn't sure that I can put it into words. It was otherworldly. It was a bit scary at times. It was supernatural. More medicinal than I would have liked. But next to the birth of my own children, which I wasn't exactly an innocent bystander of, it was the most miraculous event I have ever witnessed firsthand.

In a strange way it made me long for heaven. I caught a

glimpse of newness. New beginnings. A new family. New mercies. Actually, a lot of things are doing that for me lately. The fight my husband and I had the other day left me longing for heaven...for the next life. Or should I say, the next portion of life...when he and I won't even be able to argue, because it just won't be an option in our new existence. The disconnection with a friend leaves me longing for that not-so-far-off season when we won't even know what the reality of disconnection feels like. The dream that I fear won't come to pass now...well, it's not as heartbreaking when I realize that it just might come to pass then.

It's refreshing to look at life this way...not two separate lives...not *the now*, the what we can see; then the everlasting. But an extension of what we know of now...God's word talks of a new heaven and a new earth. We are already familiar with earth and its potential for beauty and the very tangible, earthy, spectacular, precious moments it can lend to our lives...why wouldn't God speak into our lives with what we already know? *An extension.* The bad, the evil, the cold, the hard, the rough, the unkind, the disconnection...all gone. But the good that we now see – those moments that are fleeting but you can see potential in them for how good this life is really supposed to be...we can let those moments linger. And we can let them point us to the next phase in our life...for those of us who call God 'Father' and Christ 'Savior' and Holy Spirit 'Counselor', we don't have a completely separate existence waiting for us somewhere beyond the ethereal horizon...we have a life that never ends...a life that begins with the moment we ask Christ to be our Forgiver and Leader...a life that can be filled with occasions that remind us what our hope is really all about. Hope is about the unseen, that is true...but it is not out of reach.

Personal Touch

Look for the hints, try to sneak glances into the next chapter, in the every day...the peeks of newness that you grasp, they will get you through your day at every turn, if you just let them.

Prayer

Dear God, give me eyes to see what You want and need me to see. Remind me that there is so much more going on in my life than what meets the eye. Make me mindful of the bigger picture. Amen.

39

I Don't Have Time!

Draw near to Me and I will draw near to you.
James 4:8

Question:
As much as I try, I can't seem to keep up with a consistent quiet time. Either I'm too busy or too bored. Any ideas?

Sound familiar? Do you struggle with daily devotions, especially now that you're a mom? You're not the only one! Let me share a few ideas with you, starting off with the statement, 'as much as I try'. That wording choice implies that the lion's share of your spiritual growth rests on your shoulders. That you have given it your best shot, probably time and again, and find yourself failing with each attempt. I would like to point out that because you have free will, yes, you are responsible for getting yourself into the presence of

God as often as you can and in as many ways as you can, but fortunately for all of us, God is in control of our growth. In other words, you are in charge of the process and God is in charge of the results. What is also implied in those few words 'as much as I try' is that what you are trying to do is difficult and distasteful. That it is an obligation. That it is something you dislike doing, and therefore you must force yourself to work at it. I think most of us have this image of God in the recesses of our minds that places Him with a big attendance chart tracking our quiet times, and we only get a gold star when we've spent an hour in prayer and Bible study at 5 in the morning. And we get demerits each and every time we hit the snooze alarm. My take on God is that all He really wants is for us to love Him and worship Him. All He really wants is to spend time with those He created for His pleasure - *us*. There is no attendance chart, and therefore no obligation. When we begin to view God as a Father, as a Friend, who simply wants to shower us with His love, the guilt eases up tremendously.

Now let's hit the 'I'm too busy' issue. You're too busy. Really? How much television have you watched in the past seven days? How many hours have you spent surfing the internet or checking e-mail? How much time did you spend on the phone, or shopping, or fill-in-the-blank? I would bet that ninety percent of people who claim to be too busy are either disorganized, using their time poorly, or saying they're too busy because it sounds important to say. For those of us who fall in that ninety percent camp, I would highly suggest ruthlessly going through your schedule and honestly examining your choices of activities and time-fillers, than getting rid of something that isn't adding quality to your life. Then go to your to-do list, your Day Timer, or your Palm Pilot, and schedule an appointment with God. He deserves that kind of attention and appreciation just as you would plan to get together with a friend for lunch, so why not? And for those of you who really do happen to be too busy...then, by all means, please consider eliminating something. There is no more important investment into your life and the lives of the people you interact with, than making sure you are being filled up with the love of God on a regular basis.

And now for those of you who are honest with themselves and can't help but notice that their quiet time leaves something to be desired, I say, you are not alone. Frank Laubach says, "If you are weary of some sleepy form of devotion, probably God is as weary of it as you are." My first recommendation to you would be to get really candid with God. Tell Him that you're bored, that the excitement and adventure of walking with Him has diminished. Then ask Him to 'restore the joy of your salvation'. Ask Him that when you draw near to Him, He will draw near to you. Ask Him to give you a heart that loves Him and desires Him and His word above all other things in your life. Ask Him to reveal Himself to you. Remind Him of promises in Scripture that say that if you seek Him with all your heart, He will be found by you. Invite God into your end of the process. We don't ask Him enough. Yes, you may have to try...but ask God to help you. And you may be very busy. But sift your life's activities through the fingers of God and tell me whether or not you have time for Him. And you may be bored. Ask God to light a fire within you for time with Him. Time spent with God is one of the only things that is going to last for eternity. And that is most definitely worth it.

Personal Touch

Moving onto the practicals...mix things up a bit. Get into a small group that is going to study some material you've never looked at before. Pick up a different translation of the Bible than what you're used to. Get up a few minutes early and go for a walk with Him. Start meeting God for coffee in the middle of the day. Stay up late and look up at the stars with Him. Keep some contemporary worship tapes in your car for those times when you find yourself driving alone. Come up with what I call triggers – where you take an everyday item and use it to help you remind yourself of something. For instance, I have a girlfriend, Keely. I sometimes call her 'Kee'. I'm trying to remember to pray for Kee when I have my keys in my hands. I have another friend, Parker…when I'm parking, that sometimes triggers something in me to pray for her. Doesn't always work, but even if I'm reminded to pray for them even one or two more times, that counts for something. Get a journal and start writing out your prayers – letters to God. You keep in touch with old friends this way – why not write your Heavenly Father? Jot down some phrases – promises, truths, Scripture – and place them all around your home, car, work environment, so that you are brought back to this truth – what author Brennan Manning says is the most important thing about you – that you are beloved of God.

Prayer

Dear God, things are lacking between You and I. I admit the reality is that if there's distance between us, it's me and not You…You never change. Please restore my desire for You. Please give me a heart that loves You more than anything else in my life. And when I meet with You, please show up in new ways. Amen.

40

Hearing Things

Now I will tell you new things I have not mentioned before,
secrets you have not yet heard.
Isaiah 48:6b

Have you ever heard the voice of God? I don't mean audible. And I don't mean, 'take that job', or 'don't marry that man'. I mean the nudge-in-your-heart kind of voice. It's almost a whisper. Something that you know was meant just for you from the Creator.

I have. And I want to share one of those experiences with you. I was traveling by train to Minnesota to visit a friend. Me. Alone. Ten hours. Can anyone say, *'Ahhhhh...'* I was in heaven. I spent the day reading magazines, listening to CD's, journaling, reading. And then I thought, 'okay, why don't I just sit...just look out the window and see if God has anything He wants to say to me?' So I did. And within moments, and I mean moments, I heard this: *"You're not a bad mom."* Now, I hadn't been reading about parenting. I hadn't been feeling guilty about going away for four days and leaving my children at home with their dad. In fact, to be honest, I wasn't even really thinking about Sara and Jack at the time. But, bam, that was what He had for me.

Now, how do I know that was the gentle voice of God? Because God is very intimate and very personal. He knew that I walk around my life muttering, "I'm a bad mom". (Maybe not out loud, but I sure do think it a lot.) Had the wording been, 'you're a good mom', I would have actually doubted the authenticity of the source, because He knows my heart isn't ready for *that* affirmation quite yet. He met me just where I was.

It gets better. He went on to say, "Sara and Jack adore you. And they *know* you love them. You are *not* a bad mom." And the tears began to flow. I needed to hear that. Probably more than I even knew I needed to. And I thanked my God for bending down and whispering that encouragement to me. And I thanked Him for being the kind of God who loves us so much that He takes the time to send little messages like that to us. Let me encourage you...*you are not a bad mom.* And may you enjoy the benefits of a walk so close with God that He whispers something precious into your soul today.

Personal Touch

You want to hear what God has to say to you? Guess what...you can't hear Him when you're running out the door...you can't hear Him when the kids are screaming... you can't hear Him at soccer practice. You need to slow down. You need some peace and quiet. You need to schedule some time with God. Just do it.

Prayer

Dear God, I want to hear You. You still have things to say to me. I want to know them. Please quiet my heart and help me to quiet my life. Speak, Lord…I'm listening. Amen.

41

They're Watching

Only be careful, and watch yourselves closely
so that you do not forget the things
your eyes have seen or let them slip from your heart
as long as you live.
Teach them to your children and to their children
after them.
Deuteronomy 4:9

There are days when I realize after the fact that one of those sometimes illusive teachable moment has happened – and I had no idea. A while ago, my daughter was having a meltdown in public...you know the kind, where you have to physically remove the child from the store kicking and screaming? How pleasant. Well, she's yelling things at me, within earshot of several customers and clerks, and I was cringing at what I heard (but couldn't help smiling a bit too). Because she wasn't yelling things like "I hate you, Mom!", for which I was truly grateful; instead she chose to tell me the following: "I'm disappointed in you! I'm telling Daddy about this when he gets home! You're being disobedient! *You need a consequence!"* Wonder where she got all of that?! That little girl of mine is listening to me...*and learning.*

And then there was the time when we were driving down the road and there was a man holding a sign that said, "Will work for food". Well, I felt the nudge of the Spirit to buy him lunch, so I went up to McDonald's and then drove back around again to bring it to him. It was hard to be inconspicuous as I had to stop traffic, roll down the passenger side window and sort of yell to get his attention...so Sara, of course, wanted to know what I was doing. I explained it simply and that was that – we never talked about it again. Until about six months later when we were driving down that same street and passed that corner...the man was not there this time, but my 6-year-old Sara said to me, "Mommy, do you remember that time you gave that man lunch?" And I said, 'Yes, honey, I remember', almost trembling because I had no idea she had that capacity for memory. And she said softly, "Mommy, that was so generous of you." She is watching me...*and learning.*

Personal Touch

By all means, grab those teachable moments when you see them. Remember though - cut yourself some slack when you just can't muster up a creative comeback...because they are watching you *all* of the time, and there will be another opportunity just around the bend.

Prayer

Dear God, remind me that my kids are watching and listening all the time. Remind me that I am helping to mold them into the adults they are going to be. Help me be the best role model I can for my children. Help me to teach them well and help me to love them well. Amen.

42

Where'd the Time Go?

There is a time for everything, and a season
for every activity under heaven...
a time to weep and a time to laugh, a time to mourn
and a time to dance.
Ecclesiastes 3:1,4

Okay, I'm having one of those mom moments when I cannot believe, with everything in me, that not only am I a mother of two, but time has moved by so quickly and without my permission to find that those two precious babies of mine are going into first grade and kindergarten already. I refuse to believe it actually. It just seems wrong.

Where did those days go of not being able to catch even two consecutive hours of sleep? Of nursing? Of just staring at my babies sleeping? Of being so excited when they could finally eat cheerios?! The first tooth? The first step? The first word? Or of that first playgroup, though knowing full well the social interaction that I claimed I was instilling into my children was for me way more than for them? Of my first look into the brilliance of Barney? Of moving my children up the ranks in their Sunday school classes? The first days of preschool? Or their first friends?

And now, I have talking, walking, thinking, praying, running, fully functioning children. But there are still so many firsts. I don't have to let go of that quite yet. Like uninitiated 'I love you's'. And first prayers that they come up with. And first discussions about something other than them. (They're beginning to understand that when they leave the room, the world does not get sucked into some planetary black hole...)

I told my Sara the other day how desperately I wanted her to stay just the way she is...because she already just seems too grown up for me. She said she understood how I felt, but she just had to keep growing. And she's right. They do. I can't hold them back. And I guess, really, when it comes down to it, I don't want to hold them back. I mean, if this is how amazing they both are now, I can't wait to see how they turn out along the way.

Personal Touch

What time-halters can you create today? Take a walk with the kids. Go to the park and just watch them play. Pull out some construction paper and draw some pictures of their life (then date them and put them in your hope chest). You can't slow the hands of time...but you can try to help yourself remember these moments more clearly.

Prayer

Dear God, help me remember all these moments, God! I don't want to forget how cute and sweet and precious my children are. Part of me forgets their baby days already...

help me remember. Thank You for my children. They are such amazing gifts. Amen.

43

Pulled

She sets about her work vigorously;
her arms are strong for her tasks.
Proverbs 31:17

S o Jack prays before breakfast, "Thank you, Jesus. Thank you that my sunflower has stopped growing. And thank you that Mommy is mad at Daddy for not cleaning the dishes. Thank you, Jesus. Amen." He is a stitch. And he catches everything that I say and do – even when I don't realize it.

Like the other day, I must have made mention that I had some work to do. You know what he told me? We were driving by a pretty cool park and he said to me, "If you don't take me to that park right now, I will call 911 on you and tell them that you won't take me to the park because you said you had to work." Ouch. So I took him to the park. I'm a sucker for a smartly-worded guilt trip, what can I say?

I've had an interesting month or so. I've gone back to work. (Maybe 'back' isn't the right word…can't really say I haven't been working as a stay-at-home mom these past few year…but you know what I mean.) I have a kindergartner and a first grader, and God brought an amazing opportunity my way for a part-time job at my church. The kind of job I knew I would want when I was really ready to work outside the home – like in a year or so when both of my kids would be in school all day. But as wonderful of a job as it is, and as much as I love it, I am being pulled in so many directions now. My heart (and mind and body) have been at home for seven years. I hadn't been looking for a job yet or wanting a job yet. But now, I'm out doing something new that I love. And I'm a bit scared because I'm watching myself do about a hundred things, but feel like I'm doing few of them well, let alone with excellence. Can you relate?

So here's my fear. My son feels the need to threaten to sic the police on me if I don't take him to the park – because I said I had work to do. And my daughter woke up in the middle of the night crying a couple days ago simply saying she was sad but didn't know why (because she misses me perhaps? because when I'm home, I'm so preoccupied these days?). I don't have any real answers to offer – I'm still just figuring all this out myself.

But I do know one thing for sure. God knows my fears. He saw my son desire a trip to the park with his mommy. And He saw my daughter crying in the middle of the night. And He sees my piles of work at home and church and sees my scattered mind and sees my tired body and sees my emotional upheaval. But He doesn't just *see* it all. He is standing by, waiting for an invitation to intervene and to give direction and to pour out peace.

Personal Touch

Are you feeling pulled in different directions? Are you feeling tired these days? Are you feeling scattered? Invite God into your chaotic world. He is waiting and watching and desperately wanting to help you. He may not come down and play with your kids or do your work for you or cook your family a great dinner (but wouldn't that be nice?!), but He *will* send a peace that carries you through the moment-to-moment. He guarantees it.

Prayer

Dear God, I need some of that peace. I'm just barely making it through each day. Please give me strength and energy and creativity and love for my family. Amen.

44

Rest for the Weary

*"Come to Me, all you who are weary and burdened,
and I will give you rest."*
Matthew 11:28

M om, are you tired? Do you feel like you're doing a thousand things, being pulled in a hundred directions, but not doing anything with excellence? Do you have so much on your mind that you leave Post-it® notes all around your house so you can jot down an idea or list when it comes to you? (Okay, maybe that one's just me...)

"Come to Me, all you who are weary and burdened, and I will give you rest," said Jesus in the book of Matthew.

Come...it is an invitation...a standing invitation...He offers, and we must accept...

...to Me...there is only One who would be this bold, who could offer something so perfect for our need...Christ alone.

*...all who...*I wonder if He said this with a subtle smile in His voice...He knew that not only would we all feel this way from time to time, most of us – if we are honest – live with weariness and burdens as an underlying way of life...this is an offer not just to a select few...but to each one of us.

*...are weary and burdened...*it's okay to admit it – you're tired sometimes...maybe more than you'd like to let on. You have a ton of things on your mind – some trivial...what should the kids wear for school pictures?, what should I bring for Thanksgiving?, how will we pay that dentist bill?...Some not so trivial...will my Dad survive the cancer?, will my husband keep his job?, will I be able to patch things up with my friend? He knows....

*...and I will give you rest...*Can you even imagine? How confident of Him. Almost nervy. Especially because He *does* know what our lives are like. Yet that is the one thing He felt we all needed the very most. *Rest.* I love even the sound of that word, let alone the concept. His offer to step into our circumstances, to navigate so we don't have to, to listen to our hearts so we don't have to walk through this with the weight of the world on our shoulders. He's ready and waiting. He offers something to you and to me...something that we need so desperately...a gentle yet strong dose of rest... and He is the only One who can truly propose this to us...because He is the only One who knows us completely, holds us up completely, and loves us completely.

Personal Touch

Mom, take a deep breath, and just go to Him...stop what you're doing and just go. Breathe in and whisper to yourself to 'be silent and know that He is God'...then breathe out and remind yourself that you are completely and amazingly loved. He'll meet you right there. He'll bring you rest.

Prayer

Dear God, I am tired. Like, really, completely emotionally worn out. I need something from You. I need You to be the lifter of my head and the encourager of my heart. Please pour out Your rest over my soul. Lead me beside still waters. I love You. Amen.

45

Dance with the One Who Brought You

Yet I hold this against you:
You have forsaken your first love.
Revelation 2:4

Picture yourself at a New Year's Eve ball. Right now you're thinking, *you want me to picture myself at a ball? I haven't done laundry in a week, I only think I showered sometime yesterday, my baby is crying, my toddler is throwing things at me, and I vaguely remember what my husband looks like – and you want me to picture myself at a ball?* Yes, I do. Imagine yourself at a ball. And you're dressed up, and having the time of your life, so you think. You are mingling. You are dancing with just about everyone. Everyone, that is, except the gracious host. Well, actually, what you're doing with these other people should not be considered dancing as you're stepping on their toes more than moving in a gentle, reciprocating rhythm. The host, on the other hand, has asked you to dance...in fact, you're there as his date, so the invitation to dance is an open one. But there are so many people to talk with, and so many things to do. You find yourself filling up your time with endless chatter and tasks. You are making the punch, but you realize you don't know how to make punch...you've never done it before. And you take in the fact that your dress is getting dirty and torn...well, you've never danced much before either. Not to mention alone. Dancing alone can be messy. And dangerous. And lonely. If only you would stop and take your gaze off your dress, or your feet, or the myriad of people and things pulling at you, and lock eyes with the person who not only wants your full attention, but has been giving you his this entire time. He is ready to whisper to you how to make punch, and to keep your dress – and you- looking lovely, and to show you how to dance. And he is willing to make this experience even fuller and sweeter than you thought it could ever be. You just need to take his hand and let him lead you. You just need to join him in the dance...because he is the one who wrote the music.

Personal Touch

Mom, are you dancing alone? Or with others besides the One who brought you? He wants to make your life sweet and secure and meaningful and more rhythmic. He has given you an open invitation to join Him in the dance of life. Will you accept His offer? In the midst of all the leaves turning over, commit to let God lead you through this life. Then go in peace...and enjoy the dance.

Prayer

Dear God, I want You to lead me. I want You to be my closest Friend. I accept Your offer to follow You. Help me. Amen.

46

Out of the Darkness

Then Job replied to the LORD:
"I know that you can do all things;
no plan of yours can be thwarted.
You asked, 'Who is this that obscures my counsel
without knowledge?'
Surely I spoke of things I did not understand,
things too wonderful for me to know.
Job 42: 1-3

A dear friend of mine was hurt...*very* hurt. Physically she will get back to normal soon enough. But emotionally and spiritually, she will never be the same again. This has hit me possibly harder than any other evil thing that has brushed through my life before. I felt a sadness that was new for me. It stemmed from three places...the smallest being the realization that this could actually happen to me...I am not untouchable, immortal, after all…only took me thirty plus years to come to that conclusion.

The next factor contributing to my depth of sadness is simply utter pain for what my precious friend went through, is going through, and will carry with her for the rest of her life…I can only begin to imagine and construct in my mind what I think she must be feeling…and it saddens me to my core…I can literally feel my heart hurt when I think about it.

But the largest dynamic is the one that has surprised me the most…after almost eighteen years of being a truster of God, I have found myself disappointed and, yes, even angry with my Creator. This has never been an emotion I have felt towards Him. But if I am to believe that He is sovereign – and we *are* to believe that wholeheartedly – then I must grapple with the fact that He had the choice to stop what was going to happen to my friend…but He chose not to.

The basicness of this lesson seems almost obscure…I have heard of evil before…I have known of evil before…I have watched evil unfold before my very eyes on television before, fiction and reality…but I have never seen the hand of evil so up-close before. It was almost as if I didn't really know it existed until now. Because surely God allows evil on a daily basis and I surely knew that before this moment in time. But I don't think I *really* knew it. And that was the issue that plunged me into near-depression for weeks and weeks. That was the haunting voice that kept me on the verge of tears. That was the thing that left me going through my life like when you find yourself at your destination but only your subconscious was driving and you have no idea how you got there. That was the nagging concern that stopped me from praying because I remember I'm not speaking to Him just yet.

I'd *never, ever* felt that way…that disconnected from the One who I thought would always protect me. It occurred to me that I didn't know His heart and character like I thought

I did. But then something began to change...very slowly, I might add. To be brutally honest, I'd been questioning His intentions toward those who are His. I used to think that He is always loving, always faithful, always good. But I doubted His love, faithfulness and goodness, as I pictured Him sitting by and watching my friend be violated.

What I am just now allowing myself to feel...is that His heart was breaking infinitely more than mine. That was lesson number one for me.

Lesson number two is from the book of Job. A friend of mine, who held me up emotionally and spiritually during this time, pointed out this passage to me. After everything had been stripped away and Job was violated in almost every physical and emotional way, he had this to say of his God, "I know that You can do all things; no plan of Yours can be thwarted. Surely I spoke of things I did not understand, things too wonderful for me to know. Please forgive me." I had been wrong. That was my other lesson. In our pain, can we be honest with God? Absolutely. No point in lying...He already knows what we feel. But I'm beginning to realize that I crossed the line. During this grieving period, which is not over I'm sure, I was irreverent...I was forgetful. I forgot the truths that I know. The enemy whispered things into my mind that I allowed to sway my thinking... thinking that had been built upon almost 18 years of God's Word and personal faith experiences. The enemy wanted me to doubt God's love...and he got me to do so. But, in spite of my pain, I chose not to do that anymore.

Life is hard. What a cliché...so allow me to rephrase. Life can be absolutely horrifying and heartbreaking and fragile and fatal. But (she says with shored up conviction), God *is* good. God *is* faithful. God *is* love. That is what I know. That is Truth. That is what is going to get me through, and I pray that will be what is going to pull my friend through. *God is Love.* Even when we can't see it. Bottomline.

Personal Touch

Has your heart been breaking lately? Please don't run from God during this time. Run to Him. He is the only One who can bring you healing...and that is what He came for.

Prayer

Dear God, I cannot get through this sadness. I need You so desperately to be my strength and to heal me. It feels like my heart will never be the same again. Please give me Your peace. Please put the pieces of my heart back together again. Amen.

47

Entering In

Be completely humble and gentle; be patient,
bearing with one another in love.
Ephesians 4:2

Entering in. This phrase has been hanging around in the back of my mind for a few weeks now. I have watched on three occasions recently the same lesson in three very different ways. When I think of 'entering in', I think of boldness and gentleness intertwined. I think of an un-self-consciousness and an other-awareness blending together. I think of compassion and risk merging to bring forth something really beautiful.

A month or so ago, I was a long-distant witness of someone close to me being put through a trauma. This person is even closer to my husband and I watched him, with such humility and strength, enter into this hurting person's circumstances. She lives in another country and within hours, my husband was on a plane to be with her – his sister. He didn't think of what he might find on the other side, what condition his sweet sister could be in – how uncomfortable that might be for him. He went there to be masculine strength when she needed it most. He entered in boldly and gently; with thoughts only of her, not of himself; with such desire to just be there for her, despite the pain he was feeling. What courage that took. I was so proud of him in those moments.

In the midst of that same situation, I had a friend who entered into my circumstances. Not that my sister's situation is about me…but the effects were like ripples washing over me when something is dropped into the water…and I found myself going under. This friend entered in…she brought me lemon bars of all things (because she knows I love her lemon bars), and she brought me a hug. She called me every day my husband was away just to check in. She brought us a meal when he got home. And when I was at my lowest point, she brought the gentlest of rebukes to get me back on track. She entered in boldly and gently, with thoughts of the pain I was experiencing, yet a desire to not let me move too far away from the only One who could really hold me up. I told her afterwards that I could write a whole book on friendship just through what she had done for me during that two-week period. Our friendship had already been strong…but the way she took care of my heart and soul, that just cemented it. I am so glad she risked my anger turning towards her and entered in.

And then last week, I had the unbelievable honor and privilege to be a part of a pre-screening of Mel Gibson's film, "The Passion of the Christ". Words cannot fully express what I felt during those two hours and what I have felt since. But I realized that Jesus made the ultimate act of 'entering in'. He went with gentleness and boldness, with no thought of Himself, just us – to the cross. He went where He did not have to go...but where He knew we needed Him to go. I was so struck by all He took for us. "He was wounded for our transgressions..." Oh to be able to fully understand the implications of 'wounded'. What He entered in for me...what He entered in *for you*...we will never be able to completely comprehend or to repay or to show our gratitude sufficiently. I just kept thinking as I watched this epic – '...I am so sorry...' and '...thank You so much....'. He didn't have to enter in for you or me...but, ladies, He did. He did.

Personal Touch

When was the last time you really entered into someone else's circumstances? Are you the kind of friend who can be called at 2 am for any reason? Do you want to be? Or maybe, what you need to work on is actually allowing yourself to be taken care of. It's harder than it looks. We need other people to get through this life...literally *need* them. Let yourself be taken care of. And the next time the opportunity presents itself, enter into someone's else's life. You will be so glad you did.

Prayer

Dear God, help me be the kind of friend that cares intimately about my friends. Help me to be unselfish with my time. Help me to be free with my words of encouragement. Help me to be creative in how I take care of them. And teach me to be the kind of friend You would be, so I can help my friends through the really tough stretches of life. And when it's my turn to walk through a hard season, help me to let You take care of me through my friends. Amen.

48

True Hope

*Then you will know that I am the Lord; those who hope in
me will not be disappointed.*
Isaiah 49:23

I've been thinking a lot about hope lately. Hope is an interesting concept. One that I fear is too easily thrown around in Christian circles. We all have a hope...yes, absolutely. But from what I can tell – we do not all have a hope that God will work out our earthly circumstances the way we want Him to. Our marriage may remain challenging; our cancer may not heal; the baby we dream of may not come; the life dream may not come to pass. There is no guarantee in God's Word that tells us this life will be easy or fair. Just the contrary, in fact. We are practically guaranteed that we *will* experience hardships of one kind or the other. But His word does talk about hope...just of a different kind.

Psalm 42:5 says, "Why are you downcast, O my soul? Why so disturbed within me? Put your hope in God, for I will yet praise Him, my Savior and my God." Did you catch that? The psalmist is desperately sad here. Yet he reminds himself that he will 'yet praise Him'…in other words…still praise Him anyway…in spite of his circumstances, maybe even *because of* his circumstances. That is one main response we are to have to life's hard times…praise our God, even when we don't feel like it.

Isaiah 49:23 says, "Then you will know that I am the Lord; those who hope in me will not be disappointed." Really? All I have to do is hope in God and I will not be disappointed? That may rub some of us the wrong way…I know it did me the first time I read it years ago during a really sad season of my life…'I have hoped for years, Lord – and I am very disappointed that this is how my life has turned out.' Ah ha! There's the key. John Ortberg, in his book, <u>The</u> <u>Life</u> <u>You've</u> <u>Always</u> <u>Wanted</u>, talks about the concept of 'disappointment'. Break apart that word – 'dis' means to miss; and 'appoint'…something prearranged, predetermined…an appointment. To be disappointed means to miss an appointment that has already been set. That word actually is a contradiction within itself. So when it says in Isaiah that those who hope in the Lord will not be disappointed – it means that those of us who hope in God will not miss out on the life already appointed for us, as long as our focus stays on God. And trust me, ladies, that appointed life of ours, is infinitely better than any kind of life we could hope to conger up in our own strength and with our limited, humanly vision and resources.

And Colossians 1:5 says, "…there is a faith and love that spring from the hope that is stored up for you in heaven." So this hope of ours - it is an *eternal* hope…one that is being stored up for us in heaven. In other words, life may not get fixed for us down here…only God knows if our current circumstances will ever change. But – the eternal hope we can all cling to - that hope is that if Christ is our Leader and Forgiver, we have Him standing by our side, ready to walk through any fire with us and help us get to the other side...we might not come through unscathed...*we might not even come through at all*...but we will never have to journey all alone, if Christ is our Savior. Our hope is waiting for us on the other side of this life.

Personal Touch

Are you in need of a big dose of hope these days? Are you feeling overwhelmed, to the point of desperation? You are not alone. Reach out. Reach out to your husband or to a friend or to a pastor. And make sure, above all else, that you are reaching out to God. He is holding our hope for us.

Prayer

Dear God, I need a reminder of my hope. I need spiritual eyes to see my reality. I'm hanging by a thread here...please meet me here and don't let go. Amen.

49

From the Heart

I will give you a new heart and put a new spirit in you;
I will remove from you your heart of stone
and give you a heart of flesh.
Ezekiel 36:26

I've been skimming lately. For about six months now, I think. I am living out of the shallowness that lies somewhere between the tyranny of the urgent and exhaustion, both physical and emotional. I don't like who I am when I'm this way. I tend to be an introvert, one who is quite contemplative. I like to celebrate the joys in my life and I even treasure the mourning process of the sad times of the journey. But not lately. Lately, I barely blink at the really good *or* the really bad.

But I'm waking up to something again. I know that I prefer to live from my heart. That is not only how God created me (and you as well, I'd like to add)...but it's how I enjoy living life the most. Reflective...thoughtful...meditative. It's hard – this living from the heart. Because it takes work. It takes a conscious effort on my part not to allow myself to just skim. When I respond defensively to my husband, boy is it ever easier to either write it off as PMS or as Kevin saying something that he shouldn't have. The challenge comes when I force myself to think about why I responded that way. What is under the surface that caused me to say what I said or feel what I felt? Did he unintentionally re-prick a previous wound? Do I have the guts to tell him about it? To sit with it for awhile and not just sweep all I can under the carpet for the sake of keeping false peace?

How are you doing lately? Just getting by? Or are you able to really enjoy the good that comes and really work through the bad that sets in? As a mom, I really want to pass on coping skills to my kids that don't just consist of crying, yelling, or slamming the bedroom door (all of which I am guilty of, by the way). Because there's got to be more than that. Because Christ calls me to so much more than that. He calls me to stick it out. He calls me to love. He calls me to live from my heart. He calls me to figure out where I am wounded and to come to Him for healing. He is close to the brokenhearted – and best I can tell, that is all of us in one way or the other.

So how can we live from our hearts? How can we really get out of life what we are intended to? I see only one way really. Be as connected to the Source of life as possible. You must – I must – spend time alone with God...and on a regular basis. But how? I don't have time, you are internally screaming at me. You are going to have to set aside some time...it is going to be a sacrifice. You are going to have to get up earlier or stay up later or get a sitter or ask your husband or not watch that TV show or put down that magazine or refrain from checking e-mail just one more time…you are going to have to do something differently than you normally do to carve time out. Because it is only when we slow down – and I mean slow down to a screeching halt of silence – that we will be able to hear the whispers… the wonderful things God wants to tell you *about you*. That you were specially created. That there is a bigger story and you have a part to play. That you are so loved you barely understand the half of it. But, Moms, you must slow down to bring Him your heart. But from one mom to another – you'll be so very glad that you did. He's waiting…

Personal Touch

This bears repeating…set aside time in the next week to get alone with God for even thirty minutes…an hour or more if you can spare it. The health of your soul depends on it.

Prayer

Dear God, I need time alone with You. I want to live from my heart. I don't want to live in the shallow waters of life anymore. Please teach me what my heart needs. Please give me what my heart needs. I love You. Amen.

50

Time Flies Pretty Much No Matter What You Do

There is a time for everything...
a time to weep and a time to laugh.
Ecclesiastes 3:1a, 4a

It's 2:45 in the morning. I can't fall back to sleep. And I'm nauseous. For whatever reason, I just realized, and I mean, *really* realized, that school starts in two weeks. Big deal, right? Well, this year is a bit different. My husband is a teacher, so typically, about this time, I'm sighing with a bit of relief that my normalcy is going to return. But not this year. Because this year, my daughter is entering second grade and my son first grade. They will both be in school full time.

Now, yes, there is a part of me that has been chanting

inwardly "Fall 2004" for the past seven or so years, especially on really hard mommy days. And yes, there is a part of me that cannot believe I'm going to have thirty hours a week to myself...to do whatever I want. So don't get me wrong...I'm looking forward to this new season, just with some mixed feelings and a bit of trepidation.

What is this that is making me feel like throwing up in the middle of the night with two weeks of summer to go? Eight years ago I was in the home stretch of my first pregnancy with my daughter, Sara. And now, I am sitting here wondering when eight years morphed into feeling like about two or three weeks. I remember being pregnant. I remember sitting outside getting a bit of sun, trying to soak in those last few lazy days, knowing my life was on the verge of changing forever. And now here I am, on the other side of the diaper years, heck the other side of the stay-at-home-mommy years basically, eight years later...but time did something more magical than just cliché-dly fly...it zoomed past me and took the youth of my children with it. And now they are independent, wonderful children who can handle a day at school solo. And I am left with other moms asking me if I'm excited about all the free time I'm about to have on my hands, when I'm actually thinking, 'no, I'm just very sad that the best and most precious season of my life...those hard, fun, sweet, amazing days and months and years of being at home raising my daughter and my son...are basically finished.' But that's not what I say...I just say that it'll be interesting and then I mumble something about time flying and I sigh.

So, moms...if you're reading this and your kids are young and at home with you all day every day...I cannot say this strongly enough...you are in one of the most wonderful stretches of life that you'll ever be blessed to live through...and even when the day doesn't seem like it will come to an end, it will...and one day you'll look up from your day-to-day and realize that you're walking your kids to school. Saying it goes fast doesn't even begin to describe it. It will race ahead, with your children in tow, even if you're not ready and willing. Because time really does fly.

Personal Touch

You know, we hear that cliché – 'time flies' – and we nod our heads or roll our eyes or wish it would go faster, depending on the day, how the kids have been so far, and our mood. But it's no joke — it goes fast, and there's no reclaiming those young children years. So, put down that load of laundry, or unplug that vacuum, or walk away from that computer, and do whatever you need to do to enjoy your sweet children this moment.

Prayer

Dear God, I know You won't make time stand still, but please give me an awareness, an urgency, to be 'in the moment' with my kids. Remind me what is important – them! And remind me what is not — we can fill in the blank. I want to remember my children's childhoods and want them to feel so completely loved. Please help me. Amen.

Conclusion

I have the privilege to do some public speaking to accompany my writing. I meet a lot of different women each year. And I've made a couple observations...we can have the most diverse circumstances as the backdrop of our lives – some work outside the home, some are stay-at-home moms; some are married, others single, divorced or widowed; some are financially set, some are struggling; some have one child, some may have four or five or six. But you know what I am finding – we are so very much alike. We all have the same questions running as white noise through our minds all day, every day. Am I doing a good job? Am I a good mom? Am I raising good kids? Am I normal? Am I doing anything of long-term worth? Am I ever going to find Calm? Am I beautiful? Am I good enough? Am I loved? I can see it in their eyes...when these women come talk to me after I give a message.

We all want affirmation. We all compare ourselves to others. We all lift others up and put ourselves down. We all sin. We all fall short. But, and this is my favorite part of the Story, we are all loved. I will go down with the ship saying this. If this is the only message that any woman takes away from any talk I give or any piece I write, I will be a happy girl. You...yes, you, holding this book in your hands...are so completely and dangerously and hugely and intimately and outrageously and gently loved by God. So deeply – there was only one way He could convey it with its proper weight – He allowed His Son to die a horrendous death for you. And then gave His Son power to come back to life...to fight for the freedom of your heart. Because, precious woman, you are worth it to Him. You *are* doing a good job. You *are* a good mom. You *are* raising good kids. You *are* normal. You *are* building worthwhile lives. You *can* find Calm. You *are* beautiful. You *are* good enough. You *are* loved. *God loves you.* He's fighting for you. Love Him back with all your heart, all your soul, all your mind, and all your life.

APPENDIX A

Ideas for Devotional Times

Set the mood:
- Set aside 10-15 minutes alone (more if you can).
- Have your Bible, a notebook and pencil ready.
- Light a candle.
- Begin your time with a prayer that the Spirit guide you in your time with God.

Appointment #1
- In your notebook, answer these questions as honestly as you can:
- How would you describe your spiritual walk?
- Where would you like to be?
- What do you struggle with the most?
- What questions do you keep coming up against spiritually (if any)?
- If you could change one aspect of how you live out your Christianity, what would it be?

Appointment #2
- Read John 1.

- In your notebook, write down any thoughts you have about this chapter and what you learn about Jesus here.

Appointment #3
- In your notebook, finish these sentences:
- When I think of God the Father, I...
- When I think of God the Son, I...
- When I think of God the Spirit, I...

Appointment #4
- In your notebook, list the temptations that you face.
- Brainstorm what you could do to better resist them.

Appointment #5
- Read Philippians chs. 1 & 2:1-18.
- In your notebook, write down any thoughts you have about this chapter and what you learn about Jesus here.

Appointment #6
- Read James 3:1-18.
- Write down your thoughts on prayer from this passage.
- Where are you at?

    ☐ I love to pray   ☐ I like to pray
    ☐ I struggle with prayer   ☐ Prayer? What's that?

Why do you think you checked the box that you checked?

Appointment #7
- Read Psalm 119.
- In your notebook, list all the benefits you can find to

reading and meditating (thinking and focusing on) God's Word.

Appointment #8

- Read Psalm 26:8, 27:4, 84:1-2,10. In your notebook, write them out.
- What do these verses mean to you where you're at right now in your life?

Printed in the United States
201426BV00007B/130-153/A